Cows, Pigs,
Wars, and Witches

COWS, PIGS, WARS & WITCHES

THE RIDDLES OF CULTURE

MARVIN HARRIS

VINTAGE BOOKS
A DIVISION OF RANDOM HOUSE, INC.
NEW YORK

[1989, c1974]

VINTAGE BOOKS EDITION, NOVEMBER 1989

Copyright © 1974 by Marvin Harris

Library of Congress Cataloging in Publication Data
Harris, Marvin, 1927–
    Cows, pigs, wars, and witches.

    Includes biographical references.
    1. Ethnology–Miscellanea. 2. Witchcraft.
I. Title.
[GN320.H328 1975]   /   392   74–16455
ISBN 0–679–72468–0(pbk.)

"The Song of Victory" from *The Essene Writings from Qumran* by A.
Dupont-Sommer, translated by G. Vermes. Translation copyright © 1962 by
The World Publishing Company. Reprinted by arrangement with The New
American Library Inc., New York, N. Y.

Manufactured in the United States of America
B98765

Preface

I HAD JUST finished trying to convince a class of under-
graduates that there was a rational explanation for the Hindu
taboo on cow slaughter. I was certain that I had anticipated
every conceivable objection. Beaming with confidence, I
asked if anyone had any questions. An agitated young man
raised his hand. "But what about the Jewish taboo on
pork?"

Some months later I began to do research aimed at
explaining why both the Jews and Moslems abhor pork. It
took me about a year before I was ready to try out my ideas
on a group of colleagues. As soon as I stopped talking, a
friend of mine who is an expert on South American Indians
said, "But what about the Tapirapé taboo on venison?"

And so it has gone with each of these riddles for which I
have tried to find a practical explanation. As soon as I finish

explaining one previously inscrutable custom or lifestyle, someone counters with another.

"Well, maybe that holds true for potlatch among the Kwakiutl, but how do you explain warfare among the Yanomamo?"

"I think there may be a shortage of protein there . . ."

"But what about the cargo cults in the New Hebrides?" Explanations of lifestyles are like potato chips. People insist on eating them until the whole bagful is gone.

That's one of the reasons why this book keeps moving from one subject to another. From India to the Amazon and from Jesus to Carlos Castaneda. But there are some differences as compared with the average bag of potato chips. For one thing, I advise against pulling out the first morsel that strikes your fancy. My explanation for witches depends on the explanation for messiahs and the explanation for messiahs depends on the explanation for "big men" which depends on the explanation for sexism which depends on the explanation for pig love which depends on the explanation for pig hate which depends on the explanation for cow love. Not that the world began with cow love, but in my own attempt to understand the causes of lifestyles, that's where I began. So please don't grab at random.

It's important that the chapters in this book be seen as building on each other and as having a cumulative effect. Otherwise, I will have no defense against the pummeling that experts in a dozen fields and disciplines will surely want to give me. I respect experts and want to learn from them. But they can be as much of an encumbrance as an asset if you have to depend on several of them at once. Have you ever tried to ask a specialist in Hinduism about pig love in New

Guinea, or an authority on New Guinea about pig hate among Jews, or an expert on Judaism about messiahs in New Guinea? (It is in the nature of the beast to crave only one potato chip for its entire life.)

My excuse for venturing across disciplines, continents, and centuries is that the world extends across disciplines, continents, and centuries. Nothing in nature is quite so separate as two mounds of expertise.

I respect the work of individual scholars who patiently expand and perfect their knowledge of a single century, tribe, or personality, but I think that such efforts must be made more responsive to issues of general and comparative scope. The manifest inability of our overspecialized scientific establishment to say anything coherent about the causes of lifestyles does not arise from any intrinsic lawlessness of lifestyle phenomena. Rather, I think it is the result of bestowing premium rewards on specialists who never threaten a fact with a theory. A proportionate relationship such as has existed for some time now between the volume of social research and the depth of social confusion can mean only one thing: the aggregate social function of all that research is to prevent people from understanding the causes of their social life.

The pundits of the knowledge establishment insist that this state of confusion is due to a shortage of studies. Soon there will be a seminar in the sky based on ten thousand new field trips. But we shall know less, not more, if these scholars have their way. Without a strategy aimed at bridging the gap between specialties and at organizing existing knowledge along theoretically coherent lines, additional research will not lead to a better understanding of the causes of lifestyles. If we genuinely seek casual explanations, we must have at least some rough idea about where to look among the potentially inexhaustible facts of nature and culture. I hope that my own work will someday be found to have contributed toward the development of such a strategy—toward showing where to look.

Contents

Prologue

T HIS BOOK is about the causes of apparently irrational and inexplicable lifestyles. Some of these enigmatic customs occur among preliterate or "primitive" peoples—for example, the boastful American Indian chiefs who burn their possessions to show how rich they are. Others belong to developing societies, my favorite being the Hindus who refuse to eat beef even though they're starving. Still others have to do with messiahs and witches who are part of the mainstream of our own civilization. To make my point, I have deliberately chosen bizarre and controversial cases that seem like insoluble riddles.

Ours is an age that claims to be the victim of an overdose of intellect. In a vengeful spirit, scholars are busily at work trying to show that science and reason cannot explain variations in human lifestyles. And so it is fashionable to insist that the riddles examined in the chapters to come have no solution. The ground for much of this current thinking about lifestyle enigmas was prepared by Ruth Benedict in her book *Patterns of Culture.* To explain striking differences among the cultures of the Kwakiutl, the Dobuans, and the Zuni, Benedict fell back upon a myth which she attributed to the Digger Indians. The myth said: "God gave to every people a cup, a cup of clay, and from this cup they drank their life . . . They all dipped in the water but their cups were different." What this has meant to many people ever since is that only God knows why the Kwakiutl burn their houses. Ditto for why the Hindus refrain from eating beef, or the Jews and Moslems abhor pork, or why some people believe in messiahs while others believe in witches. The long-term practical effect of this suggestion has been to discourage the search for other kinds of explanations. For one thing is clear: If you don't believe that a puzzle has an answer, you'll never find it.

To explain different patterns of culture we have to begin by assuming that human life is not merely random or capricious. Without this assumption, the temptation to give up when confronted with a stubbornly inscrutable custom or institution soon proves irresistible. Over the years I have discovered that lifestyles which others claimed were totally inscrutable actually had definite and readily intelligible causes. The main reason why these causes have been so long overlooked is that everyone is convinced that "only God knows the answer."

Another reason why many customs and institutions seem so mysterious is that we have been taught to value elaborate "spiritualized" explanations of cultural phenomena more than down-to-earth material ones. I contend that the solution to each of the riddles examined in this book lies in a better understanding of practical circumstances. I shall show that even the most bizarre-seeming beliefs and practices turn out on closer inspection to be based on ordinary, banal, one might say "vulgar" conditions, needs, and activities. What I mean by a banal or vulgar solution is that it rests on the ground and that it is built up out of guts, sex, energy, wind, rain, and other palpable and ordinary phenomena.

This does not mean that the solutions to be offered are in any sense simple or obvious. Far from it. To identify the relevant material factors in human events is always a difficult task. Practical life wears many disguises. Each lifestyle comes wrapped in myths and legends that draw attention to impractical or supernatural conditions. These wrappings give people a social identity and a sense of social purpose, but they conceal the naked truths of social life. Deceptions about the mundane causes of culture weigh upon ordinary consciousness like layered sheets of lead. It is never an easy task to circumvent, penetrate, or lift this oppressive burden.

In an age eager to experience altered, nonordinary states of consciousness, we tend to overlook the extent to which our ordinary state of mind is already a profoundly mystified consciousness—a consciousness surprisingly isolated from the practical facts of life. Why should this be?

For one thing, there is ignorance. Most people achieve awareness of only a small portion of the range of lifestyle alternatives. To emerge from myth and legend to mature consciousness we need to compare the full range of past and present cultures. Then there is fear. Against events like growing old and dying, false consciousness may be the only effective defense. And finally, there is conflict. In ordinary social life, some persons invariably control or exploit others. These inequalities are as much disguised, mystified, and lied about as old age and death.

Ignorance, fear, and conflict are the basic elements of everyday consciousness. From these elements, art and politics fashion that collective dreamwork whose function it is to prevent people from understanding what their social life is all about. Everyday consciousness, therefore, cannot explain itself. It owes its very existence to a developed capacity to deny the facts that explain its existence. We don't expect dreamers to explain their dreams; no more should we expect lifestyle participants to explain their lifestyles.

Some anthropologists and historians take the opposite view. They argue that the participants' explanation constitutes an irreducible reality. They warn that human consciousness should never be treated as an "object," and that the scientific framework appropriate to the study of physics or chemistry has no relevance when applied to the study of lifestyles. Various prophets of the modern "counter-culture" even blame the inequities and disasters of recent history on too much "objectification." One of them claims that objective consciousness always leads to a loss of "moral sensitivity," and thereby equates the quest for scientific knowledge with original sin.

Nothing could be more absurd. Hunger, war, sexism, torture, and exploitation have occurred throughout history and prehistory—long before anybody got the idea of trying to "objectify" human events.

Some people who are disillusioned with the side effects of advanced technology think that science is "the commanding lifestyle of our society." This may be accurate with respect to our knowledge of nature, but it is terribly wrong with respect to our knowledge of culture. As far as lifestyles are concerned, knowledge can't be original sin because we are still in our original state of ignorance.

But let me postpone further discussion of the claims of the counter-culture until my final chapter. Let me first show how a series of important lifestyle riddles can be given a scientific explanation. There is little to be gained by arguing about theories that are not grounded in specific facts and contexts. I ask only one indulgence. Please remember that like any scientist, I hope to present probable and reasonable solutions, not certainties. Yet imperfect as they may be, probable solutions must take precedence over no solutions at all—such as Benedict's Digger Indian myth. Like any scientist, I welcome alternative explanations, provided that they better fulfill the standards of scientific evidence and as long as they explain as much. And so—on to the riddles.

Mother Cow

WHENEVER I get into discussions about the influence of practical and mundane factors on lifestyles, someone is sure to say, "But what about all those cows the hungry peasants in India refuse to eat?" The picture of a ragged farmer starving to death alongside a big fat cow conveys a reassuring sense of mystery to Western observers. In countless learned and popular allusions, it confirms our deepest conviction about how people with inscrutable Oriental minds ought to act. It is comforting to know—somewhat like "there will always be an England"—that in India spiritual values are more precious than life itself. And at the same time it makes us feel sad. How can we ever hope to understand people so different from ourselves? Westerners find the idea that there might be a practical explanation for Hindu love of cow more upsetting than Hindus do. The sacred cow—how else can I say it?—is one of our favorite sacred cows.

Hindus venerate cows because cows are the symbol of everything that is alive. As Mary is to Christians the mother of God, the cow to Hindus is the mother of life. So there is no greater sacrilege for a Hindu than killing a cow. Even the taking of human life lacks the symbolic meaning, the unutterable defilement, that is evoked by cow slaughter.

According to many experts, cow worship is the number one cause of India's hunger and poverty. Some Western-trained agronomists say that the taboo against cow slaughter is keeping one hundred million "useless" animals alive. They claim that cow worship lowers the efficiency of agriculture because the useless animals contribute neither milk nor meat while competing for croplands and foodstuff with useful animals and hungry human beings. A study sponsored by the Ford Foundation in 1959 concluded that possibly half of India's cattle could be regarded as surplus in relation to feed supply. And an economist from the University of Pennsylvania stated in 1971 that India has thirty million unproductive cows.

It does seem that there are enormous numbers of surplus, useless, and uneconomic animals, and that this situation is a direct result of irrational Hindu doctrines. Tourists on their way through Delhi, Calcutta, Madras, Bombay, and other Indian cities are astonished at the liberties enjoyed by stray cattle. The animals wander through the streets, browse off the stalls in the market place, break into private gardens, defecate all over the sidewalks, and snarl traffic by pausing to chew their cuds in the middle of busy intersections. In the countryside, the cattle congregate on the shoulders of every highway and spend much of their time taking leisurely walks down the railroad tracks.

Love of cow affects life in many ways. Government agencies maintain old age homes for cows at which owners may board their dry and decrepit animals free of charge. In Madras, the police round up stray cattle that have fallen ill and nurse them back to health by letting them graze on small fields adjacent to the station house. Farmers regard their cows as members of the family, adorn them with garlands and tassels, pray for them when they get sick, and call in their neighbors and a priest to celebrate the birth of a new calf. Throughout India, Hindus hang on their walls calendars that portray beautiful, bejeweled young women who have the bodies of big fat white cows. Milk is shown jetting out of each teat of these half-woman, half-zebu goddesses.

Aside from the beautiful human face, cow pinups bear little resemblance to the typical cow one sees in the flesh. For most of the year their bones are their most prominant feature. Far from having milk gushing from every teat, the gaunt beasts barely manage to nurse a single calf to maturity. The average yield of whole milk from the typical hump-backed breed of zebu cow in India amounts to less than 500 pounds a year. Ordinary American dairy cattle produce over 5,000 pounds, while for champion milkers, 20,000 pounds is not unusual. But this comparison doesn't tell the whole story. In any given year about half of India's zebu cows give no milk at all—not a drop.

To make matters worse, love of cow does not stimulate love of man. Since Moslems spurn pork but eat beef, many Hindus consider them to be cow killers. Before the partition of the Indian subcontinent into India and Pakistan, bloody communal riots aimed at preventing the Moslems from killing cows became annual occurrences. Memories of old cow riots—as, for example, the one in Bihar in 1917 when thirty people died and 170 Moslem villages were looted down to the last doorpost—continue to embitter relations between India and Pakistan.

Although he deplored the rioting, Mohandas K. Gandhi was an ardent advocate of cow love and wanted a total ban on cow slaughter. When the Indian constitution was drawn up, it included a bill of rights for cows which stopped just short of outlawing every form of cow killing. Some states have since banned cow slaughter altogether, but others still permit exceptions. The cow question remains a major cause of rioting and disorders, not only between Hindus and the remnants of the Moslem community, but between the ruling Congress Party and extremist Hindu factions of cow lovers. On November 7, 1966, a mob of 120,000 people, led by a band of chanting, naked holy men draped with garlands of marigolds and smeared with white cow-dung ash, demonstrated against cow slaughter in front of the Indian House of Parliament. Eight persons were killed and forty-eight injured during the ensuing riot. This was followed by a nationwide wave of fasts among holy men, led by Muni Shustril Kumar, president of the All-Party Cow Protection Campaign Committee.

To Western observers familiar with modern industrial techniques of agriculture and stock raising, cow love seems senseless, even suicidal. The efficiency expert yearns to get his hands on all those useless animals and ship them off to a proper fate. And yet one finds certain inconsistencies in the condemnation of cow love. When I began to wonder if there might be a practical explanation for the sacred cow, I came across an intriguing government report. It said that India had too many cows but too few oxen. With so many cows around, how could there be a shortage of oxen? Oxen and male water buffalo are the principal source of traction for plowing India's fields. For each farm of ten acres or less, one pair of oxen or water buffalo is considered adequate. A little arithmetic shows that as far as plowing is concerned, there is indeed a shortage rather than a surplus of animals. India has 60 million farms, but only 80 million traction animals. If each farm had its quota of two oxen or two water buffalo, there ought to be 120 million traction animals—that is, 40 million more than are actually available.

The shortage may not be quite so bad since some farmers rent or borrow oxen from their neighbors. But the sharing of plow animals often proves impractical. Plowing must be coordinated with the monsoon rains, and by the time one farm has been plowed, the optimum moment for plowing another may already have passed. Also, after plowing is over, a farmer still needs his own pair of oxen to pull his oxcart, the mainstay of bulk transport throughout rural India. Quite possibly private ownership of farms, livestock, plows, and oxcarts lowers the efficiency of Indian agriculture, but this, I soon realized, was not caused by cow love.

The shortage of draft animals is a terrible threat that hangs over most of India's peasant families. When an ox falls sick a poor farmer is in danger of losing his farm. If he has no replacement for it, he will have to borrow money at usurious rates. Millions of rural households have in fact lost all or part of their holdings and have gone into sharecropping or day labor as a result of such debts. Every year hundreds of thousands of destitute farmers end up migrating to the cities, which already teem with unemployed and homeless persons.

The Indian farmer who can't replace his sick or deceased ox is in much the same situation as an American farmer who can neither replace nor repair his broken tractor. But there is an important difference: tractors are made by factories, but oxen are made by cows. A farmer who owns a cow owns a factory for making oxen. With or without cow love, this is a good reason for him not to be too anxious to sell his cow to the slaughterhouse. One also begins to see why Indian farmers might be willing to tolerate cows that give only 500 pounds of milk per year. If the main economic function of the zebu cow is to breed male traction animals, then there's no point in comparing her with specialized American dairy animals, whose main function is to produce milk. Still, the milk produced by zebu cows plays an important role in meeting the nutritional needs of many poor families. Even small amounts of milk products can improve the health of people who are forced to subsist on the edge of starvation.

When Indian farmers want an animal primarily for milking purposes they turn to the female water buffalo, which has longer lactation periods and higher butterfat yields than zebu cattle. Male water buffalo are also superior animals for plowing in flooded rice paddies. But oxen are more versatile and are preferred for dry-field farming and road transport. Above all, zebu breeds are remarkably rugged, and can survive the long droughts that periodically afflict different parts of India.

Agriculture is part of a vast system of human and natural relationships. To judge isolated portions of this "ecosystem" in terms that are relevant to the conduct of American agribusiness leads to some very strange impressions. Cattle

figure in the Indian ecosystem in ways that are easily overlooked or demeaned by observers from industrialized, high-
energy societies. In the United States, chemicals have almost
completely replaced animal manure as the principal source
of farm fertilizer. American farmers stopped using manure
when they began to plow with tractors rather than mules
or horses. Since tractors excrete poisons rather than fertilizers, a commitment to large-scale machine farming is
almost of necessity a commitment to the use of chemical
fertilizers. And around the world today there has in fact
grown up a vast integrated petrochemical-tractor-truck industrial complex that produces farm machinery, motorized
transport, oil and gasoline, and chemical fertilizers and
pesticides upon which new high-yield production techniques
depend.

For better or worse, most of India's farmers cannot participate in this complex, not because they worship their
cows, but because they can't afford to buy tractors. Like
other underdeveloped nations, India can't build factories
that are competitive with the facilities of the industrialized
nations nor pay for large quantities of imported industrial
products. To convert from animals and manure to tractors
and petrochemicals would require the investment of incredible amounts of capital. Moreover, the inevitable effect
of substituting costly machines for cheap animals is to reduce the number of people who can earn their living from
agriculture and to force a corresponding increase in the size
of the average farm. We know that the development of
large-scale agribusiness in the United States has meant the
virtual destruction of the small family farm. Less than 5
percent of U.S. families now live on farms, as compared

with 60 percent about a hundred years ago. If agribusiness were to develop along similar lines in India, jobs and housing would soon have to be found for a quarter of a billion displaced peasants.

Since the suffering caused by unemployment and homelessness in India's cities is already intolerable, an additional massive build-up of the urban population can only lead to unprecedented upheavals and catastrophes.

With this alternative in view, it becomes easier to understand low-energy, small-scale, animal-based systems. As I have already pointed out, cows and oxen provide low-energy substitutes for tractors and tractor factories. They also should be credited with carrying out the functions of a petrochemical industry. India's cattle annually excrete about 700 million tons of recoverable manure. Approximately half of this total is used as fertilizer, while most of the remainder is burned to provide heat for cooking. The annual quantity of heat liberated by this dung, the Indian housewife's main cooking fuel, is the thermal equivalent of 27 million tons of kerosene, 35 million tons of coal, or 68 million tons of wood. Since India has only small reserves of oil and coal and is already the victim of extensive deforestation, none of these fuels can be considered practical substitutes for cow dung. The thought of dung in the kitchen may not appeal to the average American, but Indian women regard it as a superior cooking fuel because it is finely adjusted to their domestic routines. Most Indian dishes are prepared with clarified butter known as *ghee,* for which cow dung is the preferred source of heat since it burns with a clean, slow, long-lasting flame that doesn't scorch the food. This enables the Indian housewife to start cooking

18

her meals and to leave them unattended for several hours while she takes care of the children, helps out in the fields, or performs other chores. American housewives achieve a similar effect through a complex set of electronic controls that come as expensive options on late-model stoves.

Cow dung has at least one other major function. Mixed with water and made into a paste, it is used as a household flooring material. Smeared over a dirt floor and left to harden into a smooth surface, it keeps the dust down and can be swept clean with a broom.

Because cattle droppings have so many useful properties, every bit of dung is carefully collected. Village small fry are given the task of following the family cow around and of bringing home its daily petrochemical output. In the cities, sweeper castes enjoy a monopoly on the dung deposited by strays and earn their living by selling it to housewives.

From an agribusiness point of view, a dry and barren cow is an economic abomination. But from the viewpoint of the peasant farmer, the same dry and barren cow may be a last desperate defense against the moneylenders. There is always the chance that a favorable monsoon may restore the vigor of even the most decrepit specimen and that she will fatten up, calve, and start giving milk again. This is what the farmer prays for; sometimes his prayers are answered. In the meantime, dung-making goes on. And so one gradually begins to understand why a skinny old hag of a cow still looks beautiful in the eyes of her owner.

Zebu cattle have small bodies, energy-storing humps on their back, and great powers of recuperation. These features are adapted to the specific conditions of Indian agriculture.

The native breeds are capable of surviving for long periods with little food or water and are highly resistant to diseases that afflict other breeds in tropical climates. Zebu oxen are worked as long as they continue to breathe. Stuart Odend'hal, a veterinarian formerly associated with Johns Hopkins University, performed field autopsies on Indian cattle which had been working normally a few hours before their deaths but whose vital organs were damaged by massive lesions. Given their enormous recuperative powers, these beasts are never easily written off as completely "useless" while they are still alive.

But sooner or later there must come a time when all hope of an animal's recovery is lost and even dung-making ceases. And still the Hindu farmer refuses to kill it for food or sell it to the slaughterhouse. Isn't this incontrovertible evidence of a harmful economic practice that has no explanation apart from the religious taboos on cow slaughter and beef consumption?

No one can deny that cow love mobilizes people to resist cow slaughter and beef eating. But I don't agree that the anti-slaughter and beef-eating taboos necessarily have an adverse effect on human survival and well-being. By slaughtering or selling his aged and decrepit animals, a farmer might earn a few more rupees or temporarily improve his family's diet. But in the long run, his refusal to sell to the slaughterhouse or kill for his own table may have beneficial consequences. An established principle of ecological analysis states that communities of organisms are adapted not to average but to extreme conditions. The relevant situation in India is the recurrent failure of the monsoon rains. To evaluate the economic significance of the anti-slaughter and anti-

Mother Cow

beef-eating taboos, we have to consider what these taboos mean in the context of periodic droughts and famine.

The taboo on slaughter and beef eating may be as much a product of natural selection as the small bodies and fantastic recuperative powers of the zebu breeds. During droughts and famines, farmers are severely tempted to kill or sell their livestock. Those who succumb to this temptation seal their doom, even if they survive the drought, for when the rains come, they will be unable to plow their fields. I want to be even more emphatic: Massive slaughter of cattle under the duress of famine constitutes a much greater threat to aggregate welfare than any likely miscalculation by particular farmers concerning the usefulness of their animals during normal times. It seems probable that the sense of unutterable profanity elicited by cow slaughter has its roots in the excruciating contradiction between immediate needs and long-run conditions of survival. Cow love with its sacred symbols and holy doctrines protects the farmer against calculations that are "rational" only in the short term. To Western experts it looks as if "the Indian farmer would rather starve to death than eat his cow." The same kinds of experts like to talk about the "inscrutable Oriental mind" and think that "life is not so dear to the Asian masses." They don't realize that the farmer would rather eat his cow than starve, but that he will starve if he does eat it.

Even with the assistance of the holy laws and cow love, the temptation to eat beef under the duress of famine sometimes proves irresistible. During World War II, there was a great famine in Bengal caused by droughts and the Japanese occupation of Burma. Slaughter of cows and draft animals reached such alarming levels in the summer of 1944 that the British had to use troops to enforce the cow-protection laws. In 1967 *The New York Times* reported:

Hindus facing starvation in the drought-stricken area of Bihar are slaughtering cows and eating the meat even though the animals are sacred to the Hindu religion.

Observers noted that "the misery of the people was beyond imagination."

The survival into old age of a certain number of absolutely useless animals during good times is part of the price that must be paid for protecting useful animals against slaughter during bad times. But I wonder how much is actually lost because of the prohibition on slaughter and the taboo on beef. From a Western agribusiness viewpoint, it seems irrational for India not to have a meat-packing industry. But the actual potential for such an industry in a country like India is very limited. A substantial rise in beef production would strain the entire ecosystem, not because of cow love but because of the laws of thermodynamics. In any food chain, the interposition of additional animal links results in a sharp decrease in the efficiency of food production. The caloric value of what an animal has eaten is always much greater than the caloric value of its body. This means that more calories are available per capita when plant food is eaten directly by a human population than when it is used to feed domesticated animals.

Because of the high level of beef consumption in the United States, three-quarters of all our croplands are used for feeding cattle rather than people. Since the per capita calorie intake in India is already below minimum daily requirements, switching croplands to meat production could only result in higher food prices and a further deterioration in the living standards for poor families. I doubt if more than 10 percent of the Indian people will ever be able to make beef an important part of their diet, regardless of whether they believe in cow love or not.

I also doubt that sending more aged and decrepit animals to existing slaughterhouses would result in nutritional gains for the people who need it most. Most of these animals get eaten anyway, even if they aren't sent to the slaughterhouse, because throughout India there are low-ranking castes whose members have the right to dispose of the bodies of dead cattle. In one way or another, twenty million cattle die every year, and a large portion of their meat is eaten by these carrion-eating "untouchables."

My friend Dr. Joan Mencher, an anthropologist who has worked in India for many years, points out that the existing slaughterhouses cater to urban middle-class non-Hindus. She notes that "the untouchables get their food in other ways. It is good for the untouchable if a cow dies of starvation in a village, but not if it gets sent to an urban slaughterhouse to be sold to Muslims or Christians." Dr. Mencher's informants at first denied that any Hindu would eat beef, but when they learned that "upper-caste" Americans liked steak, they readily confessed their taste for beef curry.

Like everything else I have been discussing, meat eating by untouchables is finely adjusted to practical conditions. The meat-eating castes also tend to be the leather-working castes, since they have the right to dispose of the skin of the fallen cattle. So despite cow love, India manages to have a huge leathercraft industry. Even in death, apparently useless animals continue to be exploited for human purposes.

I could be right about cattle being useful for traction, fuel, fertilizer, milk, floor covering, meat, and leather, and still misjudge the ecological and economic significance of the whole complex. Everything depends on how much all of this costs in natural resources and human labor relative to alternative modes of satisfying the needs of India's huge population. These costs are determined largely by what the cattle eat. Many experts assume that man and cow are locked in a deadly competition for land and food crops. This might be true if Indian farmers followed the American agribusiness model and fed their animals on food crops. But the shameless truth about the sacred cow is that she is an indefatigable scavenger. Only an insignificant portion of the food consumed by the average cow comes from pastures and food crops set aside for their use.

This ought to have been obvious from all those persistent reports about cows wandering about and snarling traffic. What are those animals doing in the markets, on the lawns, along the highways and railroad tracks, and up on the barren hillsides? What are they doing if not eating every morsel of grass, stubble, and garbage that cannot be directly consumed by human beings and converting it into milk and other useful products! In his study of cattle in West Bengal, Dr. Odend'-hal discovered that the major constituent in the cattle's diet is inedible by-products of human food crops, principally rice straw, wheat bran, and rice husks. When the Ford Foundation estimated that half of the cattle were surplus in relation to feed supply, they meant to say that half of the cattle manage to survive even without access to fodder crops. But this is an understatement. Probably less than 20 percent of what the cattle eat consists of humanly edible substances; most of this is fed to working oxen and water buffalo rather than to dry and barren cows. Odend'hal found that in his study area there was no competition between cattle and humans for land or the food supply: "Basically, the cattle convert items of little direct human value into products of immediate utility."

One reason why cow love is so often misunderstood is that it has different implications for the rich and the poor. Poor farmers use it as a license to scavenge while the wealthy farmers resist it as a rip-off. To the poor farmer, the cow is a holy beggar; to the rich farmer, it's a thief. Occasionally the cows invade someone's pastures or planted fields. The landlords complain, but the poor peasants plead ignorance and depend on cow love to get their animals back. If there is competition, it is between man and man or caste and caste, not between man and beast.

City cows also have owners who let them scrounge by day and call them back at night to be milked. Dr. Mencher recounts that while she lived for a while in a middle-class neighborhood in Madras her neighbors were constantly complaining about "stray" cows breaking into the family compounds. The strays were actually owned by people who lived in a room above a shop and who sold milk door to door in the neighborhood. As for the old age homes and police cowpounds, they serve very nicely to reduce the risk of maintaining cows in a city environment. If a cow stops producing milk, the owner may decide to let it wander around until the police pick it up and bring it to the precinct house. When the cow has recovered, the owner pays a small fine and returns it to its usual haunts. The old age homes operate on a similar principle, providing cheap government-subsidized pasture that would otherwise not be available to city cows.

Incidentally, the preferred form of purchasing milk in the cities is to have the cow brought to the house and milked on the spot. This is often the only way that the householder can be sure that he is buying pure milk rather than milk mixed with water or urine.

What seems most incredible about these arrangements is that they have been interpreted as evidence of wasteful, anti-economic Hindu practices, while in fact they reflect a degree of economizing that goes far beyond Western, "Protestant" standards of savings and husbandry. Cow love is perfectly compatible with a merciless determination to get the literal last drop of milk out of the cow. The man who takes the cow door to door brings along a dummy calf made out of stuffed calfskin which he sets down beside the cow to trick it into performing. When this doesn't work, the owner may resort to *phooka*, blowing air into the cow's uterus through a hollow pipe, or *doom dev*, stuffing its tail into the vaginal orifice. Gandhi believed that cows were treated more cruelly in India than anywhere else in the world. "How we bleed her to take the last drop of milk from her," he lamented. "How we starve her to emaciation, how we ill-treat the calves, how we deprive them of their portion of milk, how cruelly we treat the oxen, how we castrate them, how we beat them, how we overload them."

No one understood better than Gandhi that cow love had different implications for rich and poor. For him the cow was a central focus of the struggle to rouse India to authentic nationhood. Cow love went along with small-scale farming, making cotton thread on a hand spinning wheel, sitting cross-legged on the floor, dressing in a loincloth, vegetarianism, reverence for life, and strict nonviolence. To these themes Gandhi owed his vast popular following among the peasant masses, urban poor, and untouchables. It was his way of protecting them against the ravages of industrialization.

The asymmetrical implications of *ahimsa* for rich and poor are ignored by economists who want to make Indian agriculture more efficient by slaughtering "surplus" animals. Professor Alan Heston, for example, accepts the fact that the cattle perform vital functions for which substitutes are not readily available. But he proposes that the same functions could be carried out more efficiently if there were 30 million fewer cows. This figure is based on the assumption that with adequate care only 40 cows per 100 male animals would be needed to replace the present number of oxen. Since there are 72 million adult male cattle, by this formula, 24 million breeding females ought to be sufficient. Actually, there are 54 million cows. Subtracting 24 million from 54 million, Heston arrives at the estimate of 30 million "useless" animals to be slaughtered. The fodder and feed that these "useless" animals have been consuming are to be distributed among the remaining animals, who will become healthier and therefore will be able to keep total milk and dung production at or above previous levels. But whose cows are to be sacrificed? About 43 percent of the total cattle population is found on the poorest 62 percent of the farms. These farms, consisting of five acres or less, have only 5 percent of the pasture and grazing land. In other words, most of the animals that are temporarily dry, barren, and feeble are owned by the people who live on the smallest and poorest farms. So that when the economists talk about getting rid of 30 million cows, they are really talking about getting rid of 30 million cows that belong to poor families, not rich ones. But most poor families own only one cow, so what this economizing boils down to is not so much getting rid of 30 million cows as getting rid of 150 million people—forcing them off the land and into the cities.

Cow-slaughter enthusiasts base their recommendation on an understandable error. They reason that since the farmers refuse to kill their animals, and since there is a religious taboo against doing so, therefore it is the taboo that is mainly responsible for the high ratio of cows to oxen. Their error is hidden in the observed ratio itself: 70 cows to 100 oxen. If cow love prevents farmers from killing cows that are economically useless, how is it there are 30 percent fewer cows than oxen? Since approximately as many female as male animals are born, something must be causing the death of more females than males. The solution to this puzzle is that while no Hindu farmer deliberately slaughters a female calf or decrepit cow with a club or a knife, he can and does get rid of them when they become truly useless from his point of view. Various methods short of direct slaughter are employed. To "kill" unwanted calves, for example, a triangular wooden yoke is placed about their necks so that when they try to nurse they jab the cow's udder and get kicked to death. Older animals are simply tethered on short ropes and allowed to starve—a process that does not take too long if the animal is already weak and diseased. Finally, unknown numbers of decrepit cows are surreptitiously sold through a chain of Moslem and Christian middlemen and end up in the urban slaughterhouses.

If we want to account for the observed proportions of cows to oxen, we must study rain, wind, water, and land-tenure patterns, not cow love. The proof of this is that the proportion of cows to oxen varies with the relative importance of different components of the agricultural system in different regions of India. The most important variable is the amount of irrigation water available for the cultivation of rice. Wherever there are extensive wet rice paddies, the water buffalo tends to be the preferred traction animal, and the female water buffalo is then substituted for the zebu cow as a source of milk. That is why in the vast plains of northern India, where the melting Himalayan snows and monsoons create the Holy River Ganges, the proportion of cows to oxen drops down to 47 to 100. As the distinguished Indian economist K. N. Raj has pointed out, districts in the Ganges Valley where continuous year-round rice-paddy cultivation is practiced, have cow-to-oxen ratios that approach the theoretical optimum. This is all the more remarkable since the region in question—the Gangetic plain—is the heartland of the Hindu religion and contains its most holy shrines.

The theory that religion is primarily responsible for the high proportion of cows to oxen is also refuted by a comparison between Hindu India and Moslem West Pakistan. Despite the rejection of cow love and the beef-slaughter and beef-eating taboos, West Pakistan as a whole has 60 cows for every 100 male animals, which is considerably higher than the average for the intensely Hindu Indian state of Uttar Pradesh. When districts in Uttar Pradesh are selected for the importance of water buffalo and canal irrigation and compared with ecologically similar districts in West Pakistan, ratios of female to male cattle turn out to be virtually the same.

Do I mean to say that cow love has no effect whatsoever

on the cattle sex ratio or on other aspects of the agricultural system? No. What I am saying is that cow love is an active element in a complex, finely articulated material and cultural order. Cow love mobilizes the latent capacity of human beings to persevere in a low-energy ecosystem in which there is little room for waste or indolence. Cow love contributes to the adaptive resilience of the human population by preserving temporarily dry or barren but still useful animals; by discouraging the growth of an energy-expensive beef industry; by protecting cattle that fatten in the public domain or at landlord's expense; and by preserving the recovery potential of the cattle population during droughts and famines. As in any natural or artificial system, there is some slippage, friction, or waste associated with these complex interactions. Half a billion people, animals, land, labor, political economy, soil, and climate are all involved. The slaughter enthusiasts claim that the practice of letting cows breed indiscriminately and then thinning their numbers through neglect and starvation is wasteful and inefficient. I do not doubt that this is correct, but only in a narrow and relatively insignificant sense. The savings that an agricultural engineer might achieve by getting rid of an unknown number of absolutely useless animals must be balanced against catastrophic losses for the marginal peasants, especially during droughts and famines, if cow love ceases to be a holy duty.

Since the effective mobilization of all human action depends upon the acceptance of psychologically compelling creeds and doctrines, we have to expect that economic systems will always oscillate under and over their points of optimum efficiency. But the assumption that the whole system can be made to work better simply by attacking its consciousness is naïve and dangerous. Major improvements in the present system can be achieved by stabilizing India's human population, and by making more land, water, oxen, and water buffalo available to more people on a more equitable basis. The alternative is to destroy the present system and replace it with a completely new set of demographic, technological, politico-economic, and ideological relationships—a whole new ecosystem. Hinduism is undoubtedly a conservative force, one that makes it more difficult for the "development" experts and "modernizing" agents to destroy the old system and to replace it with a high-energy industrial and agribusiness complex. But if you think that a high-energy industrial and agribusiness complex will necessarily be more "rational" or "efficient" than the system that now exists, forget it.

Contrary to expectations, studies of energy costs and energy yields show that India makes more efficient use of its cattle than the United States does. In Singur district in West Bengal, Dr. Odend'hal discovered that the cattle's gross energetic efficiency, defined as the total of useful calories produced per year divided by the total calories consumed during the same period, was 17 percent. This compares with a gross energetic efficiency of less than 4 percent for American beef cattle raised on Western range land. As Odend'hal says, the relatively high efficiency of the Indian cattle complex comes about not because the animals are particularly productive, but because of scrupulous product utilization by humans: "The villagers are extremely utilitarian and nothing is wasted."

Wastefulness is more a characteristic of modern agribusiness than of traditional peasant economies. Under the new system of automated feed-lot beef production in the United States, for example, cattle manure not only goes unused, but it is allowed to contaminate ground water over wide areas and contributes to the pollution of nearby lakes and streams.

The higher standard of living enjoyed by the industrial nations is not the result of greater productive efficiency, but of an enormously expanded increase in the amount of energy available per person. In 1970 the United States used up the energy equivalent of twelve tons of coal per inhabitant, while the corresponding figure for India was one-fifth ton per inhabitant. The way this energy was expended involved far more energy being wasted per person in the United States than in India. Automobiles and airplanes are faster than oxcarts, but they do not use energy more efficiently. In fact, more calories go up in useless heat and smoke during a single day of traffic jams in the United States than is wasted by all the cows of India during an entire year. The comparison is even less favorable when we consider the fact that the stalled vehicles are burning up irreplaceable reserves of petroleum that it took the earth tens of millions of years to accumulate. If you want to see a real sacred cow, go out and look at the family car.

Pig Lovers
and Pig Haters

EVERYONE knows examples of apparently irrational food habits. Chinese like dog meat but despise cow milk; we like cow milk but we won't eat dogs; some tribes in Brazil relish ants but despise venison. And so it goes around the world.

The riddle of the pig strikes me as a good follow-up to mother cow. It presents the challenge of having to explain why certain people should hate, while others love, the very same animal.

The half of the riddle that pertains to pig haters is well known to Jews, Moslems, and Christians. The god of the ancient Hebrews went out of His way (once in the Book of Genesis and again in Leviticus) to denounce the pig as unclean, a beast that pollutes if it is tasted or touched. About 1,500 years later, Allah told His prophet Mohammed that the status of swine was to be the same for the followers of Islam. Among millions of Jews and hundreds of millions of Moslems, the pig remains an abomination, despite the fact that it can convert grains and tubers into high-grade fats and protein more efficiently than any other animal.

Less commonly known are the traditions of the fanatic pig lovers. The pig-loving center of the world is located in New Guinea and the South Pacific Melanesian islands. To the village-dwelling horticultural tribes of this region, swine are holy animals that must be sacrified to the ancestors and eaten on all important occasions, such as marriages and funerals. In many tribes, pigs must be sacrified to declare war and to make peace. The tribesmen believe that their departed ancestors crave pork. So overwhelming is the hunger for pig flesh among both the living and the dead that from time to time huge feasts are organized and almost all of a tribe's pigs are eaten at once. For several days in a row, the villagers and their guests gorge on great quantities of pork, vomiting what they cannot digest in order to make room for more. When it is all over, the pig herd is so reduced in size that years of painstaking husbandry are needed to rebuild it. No sooner is this accomplished than preparations are made for another gluttonous orgy. And so the bizarre cycle of apparent mismanagement goes on.

I shall begin with the problem of the Jewish and Islamic pig haters. Why should gods so exalted as Jahweh and Allah have bothered to condemn a harmless and even laughable beast whose flesh is relished by the greater part of mankind? Scholars who accept the biblical and Koranic condemnation of swine have offered a number of explanations. Before the Renaissance, the most popular was that the pig is literally a dirty animal—dirtier than others because it wallows in its own urine and eats excrement. But linking physical uncleanliness to religious abhorrence leads to inconsistencies. Cows that are kept in a confined space also splash about in their own urine and feces. And hungry cows will eat human excrement with gusto. Dogs and chickens do the same thing without getting anyone very upset, and the ancients must have known that pigs raised in clean pens make fastidious house pets. Finally, if we invoke purely aesthetic standards of "cleanliness," there is the formidable inconsistency that the Bible classifies locusts and grasshoppers as "clean." The argument that insects are aesthetically more wholesome than pigs will not advance the cause of the faithful.

These inconsistencies were recognized by the Jewish rabbinate at the beginning of the Renaissance. To Moses Maimonides, court physician to Saladin during the twelfth century in Cairo, Egypt, we owe the first naturalistic explanation of the Jewish and Moslem rejection of pork. Maimonides said that God had intended the ban on pork as a public health measure. Swine's flesh "has a bad and damaging effect upon the body," wrote the rabbi. Maimonides was none too specific about the medical reasons for this opinion, but he was the emperor's physician, and his judgment was widely respected.

In the middle of the nineteenth century, the discovery that trichinosis was caused by eating undercooked pork was interpreted as a precise verification of the wisdom of Maimonides. Reform-minded Jews rejoiced in the rational substratum of the biblical codes and promptly renounced the taboo on pork. If properly cooked, pork is not a menace to public health, and so its consumption cannot be offensive to God. This provoked rabbis of more fundamentalist persuasion to launch a counterattack against the entire naturalistic tradition. If Jahweh had merely wanted to protect the health of

His people, He would have instructed them to eat only well-cooked pork rather than no pork at all. Clearly, it is argued, Jahweh had something else in mind—something more important than mere physical well-being.

In addition to this theological inconsistency, Maimonides' explanation suffers from medical and epidemiological contradictions. The pig is a vector for human disease, but so are other domestic animals freely consumed by Moslems and Jews. For example, undercooked beef is a source of parasites, notably tapeworms, which can grow to a length of sixteen to twenty feet within a man's intestines, induce severe anemia, and lower resistance to other infectious diseases. Cattle, goats, and sheep are also vectors for brucellosis, a common bacterial infection in underdeveloped countries that is accompanied by fever, chills, sweats, weakness, pain, and aches. The most dangerous form is *Brucellosis melitensis*, transmitted by goats and sheep. Its symptoms are lethargy, fatigue, nervousness, and mental depression often mistaken for psychoneurosis. Finally, there is anthrax, a disease transmitted by cattle, sheep, goats, horses, and mules, but not by pigs. Unlike trichinosis, which seldom has fatal consequences and which does not even produce symptoms in the majority of infected individuals, anthrax often runs a rapid course that begins with body boils and terminates in death through blood poisoning. The great epidemics of anthrax that formerly swept across Europe and Asia were not brought under control until the development of the anthrax vaccine by Louis Pasteur in 1881.

Jahweh's failure to interdict contact with the domesticated vectors of anthrax is especially damaging to Maimonides' explanation, since the relationship between this disease in animals and man was known during biblical times. As described in the Book of Exodus, one of the plagues sent against the Egyptians clearly relates the symptomology of animal anthrax to a human disease:

... and it became a boil breaking forth with blains upon man and beast. And the magicians could not stand before Moses because of the boils, for the boils were upon the magicians, and upon all the Egyptians.

Faced with these contradictions, most Jewish and Moslem theologians have abandoned the search for a naturalistic basis of pig hatred. A frankly mystical stance has recently gained favor, in which the grace afforded by conformity to dietary taboos is said to depend upon not knowing exactly what Jahweh had in mind and in not trying to find out.

Modern anthropological scholarship has reached a similar impasse. For example, with all his faults, Moses Maimonides was closer to an explanation than Sir James Frazer, renowned author of *The Golden Bough*. Frazer declared that pigs, like "all so-called unclean animals, were originally sacred; the reason for not eating them was that many were originally divine." This is of no help whatsoever, since sheep, goats, and cows were also once worshiped in the Middle East, and yet their meat is much enjoyed by all ethnic and religious groups in the region. In particular, the cow, whose golden calf was worshiped at the foot of Mt. Sinai, would seem by Frazer's logic to make a more logical unclean animal for the Hebrews than the pig.

Other scholars have suggested that pigs, along with the rest of the animals tabooed in the Bible and the Koran, were once the totemic symbols of different tribal clans. This may very well have been the case at some remote point in history, but if we grant that possibility, we must also grant that "clean" animals such as cattle, sheep, and goats might also have served as totems. Contrary to much writing on the subject of totemism, totems are usually not animals valued as a food resource. The most popular totems among primitive clans in Australia and Africa are relatively useless birds like ravens and finches, or insects like gnats, ants, and mosquitoes, or even inanimate objects like clouds and boulders. Moreover, even when a valuable animal is a totem, there is no invariant rule that requires its human associates to refrain from eating it. With so many options available, saying that the pig was a totem doesn't explain anything. One might as well declare: "The pig was tabooed because it was tabooed."

I prefer Maimonides' approach. At least the rabbi tried to understand the taboo by placing it in a natural context of health and disease where definite mundane and practical forces were at work. The only trouble was that his view of the relevant conditions of pig hate was constrained by a physician's typical narrow concern with bodily pathology.

The solution to the riddle of the pig requires us to adopt a much broader definition of public health, one that includes the essential processes by which animals, plants, and people manage to coexist in viable natural and cultural communities. I think that the Bible and the Koran condemned the pig because pig farming was a threat to the integrity of the basic cultural and natural ecosystems of the Middle East.

To begin with, we must take into account the fact that the protohistoric Hebrews—the children of Abraham, at the turn of the second millennium B.C.—were culturally adapted to life in the rugged, sparsely inhabited arid areas between the

40

river valleys of Mesopotamia and Egypt. Until their conquest of the Jordan Valley in Palestine, beginning in the thirteenth century B.C., the Hebrews were nomadic pastoralists, living almost entirely from herds of sheep, goats, and cattle. Like all pastoral peoples they maintained close relationships with the sedentary farmers who held the oases and the great rivers. From time to time these relationships matured into a more sedentary, agriculturally oriented lifestyle. This appears to have been the case with Abraham's descendants in Mesopotamia, Joseph's followers in Egypt, and Isaac's followers in the western Negev. But even during the climax of urban and village life under King David and King Solomon, the herding of sheep, goats, and cattle continued to be a very important economic activity.

Within the overall pattern of this mixed farming and pastoral complex, the divine prohibition against pork constituted a sound ecological strategy. The nomadic Israelites could not raise pigs in their arid habitats, while for the semi-sedentary and village farming populations, pigs were more of a threat than an asset.

The basic reason for this is that the world zones of pastoral nomadism correspond to unforested plains and hills that are too arid for rainfall agriculture and that cannot easily be irrigated. The domestic animals best adapted to these zones are the ruminants—cattle, sheep, and goats. Ruminants have sacks anterior to their stomachs which enable them to digest grass, leaves, and other foods consisting mainly of cellulose more efficiently than any other mammals.

The pig, however, is primarily a creature of forests and shaded riverbanks. Although it is omnivorous, its best weight gain is from food low in cellulose—nuts, fruits, tubers, and especially grains, making it a direct competitor of man. It cannot subsist on grass alone, and nowhere in the world do fully nomadic pastoralists raise significant numbers of pigs. The pig has the further disadvantage of not being a practical source of milk and of being notoriously difficult to herd over long distances.

Above all, the pig is thermodynamically ill-adapted to the hot, dry climate of the Negev, the Jordan Valley, and the other lands of the Bible and the Koran. Compared to cattle, goats, and sheep, the pig has an inefficient system for regulating its body temperature. Despite the expression "To sweat like a pig," it has recently been proved that pigs can't sweat at all. Human beings, the sweatiest of all mammals, cool themselves by evaporating as much as 1,000 grams of body liquid per hour from each square meter of body surface. The best the pig can manage is 30 grams per square meter. Even sheep evaporate twice as much body liquid through their skins as pigs. Sheep also have the advantage of thick white wool that both reflects the sun's rays and provides insulation when the temperature of the air rises above that of the body. According to L. E. Mount of the Agricultural Research Council Institute of Animal Physiology in Cambridge, England, adult pigs will die if exposed to direct sunlight and air temperatures over 98° F. In the Jordan Valley, air temperatures of 110° F. occur almost every summer, and there is intense sunshine throughout the year.

To compensate for its lack of protective hair and its inability to sweat, the pig must dampen its skin with external moisture. It prefers to do this by wallowing in fresh clean mud, but it will cover its skin with its own urine and feces if nothing else is available. Below 84° F., pigs kept in pens deposit their excreta away from their sleeping and feeding areas, while above 84° F. they begin to excrete indiscriminately throughout the pen. The higher the temperature, the "dirtier" they become. So there is some truth to the theory that the religious uncleanliness of the pig rests upon actual physical dirtiness. Only it is not in the nature of the pig to be dirty everywhere; rather it is in the nature of the hot, arid habitat of the Middle East to make the pig maximally dependent upon the cooling effect of its own excrement.

Sheep and goats were the first animals to be domesticated in the Middle East, possibly as early as 9,000 B.C. Pigs were domesticated in the same general region about 2,000 years later. Bone counts conducted by archeologists at early prehistoric village farming sites show that the domesticated pig was almost always a relatively minor part of the village fauna, constituting only about 5 percent of the food animal remains. This is what one would expect of a creature which had to be provided with shade and mudholes, couldn't be milked, and ate the same food as man.

As I pointed out in the case of the Hindu prohibition on beef, under preindustrial conditions, any animal that is raised primarily for its meat is a luxury. This generalization applies as well to preindustrial pastoralists, who seldom exploit their herds primarily for meat.

Among the ancient mixed farming and pastoralist communities of the Middle East, domestic animals were valued primarily as sources of milk, cheese, hides, dung, fiber, and traction for plowing. Goats, sheep, and cattle provided ample amounts of these items plus an occasional supplement of lean meat. From the beginning, therefore, pork must have been a luxury food, esteemed for its succulent, tender, and fatty qualities.

Between 7,000 and 2,000 B.C. pork became still more of a luxury. During this period there was a sixtyfold increase in the human population of the Middle East. Extensive deforestation accompanied the rise in population, especially as a result of permanent damage caused by the large herds of sheep and goats. Shade and water, the natural conditions appropriate for pig raising, became progressively more scarce, and pork became even more of an ecological and economic luxury.

As in the case of the beef-eating taboo, the greater the temptation, the greater the need for divine interdiction. This relationship is generally accepted as suitable for explaining why the gods are always so interested in combating sexual temptations such as incest and adultery. Here I merely apply it to a tempting food. The Middle East is the wrong place to raise pigs, but pork remains a succulent treat. People always find it difficult to resist such temptations on their own. Hence Jahweh was heard to say that swine were unclean, not only as food, but to the touch as well. Allah was heard to repeat the same message for the same reason: It was ecologically maladaptive to try to raise pigs in substantial numbers. Small-scale production would only increase the temptation. Better then, to interdict the consumption of pork entirely, and to concentrate on raising goats, sheep, and cattle. Pigs tasted good but it was too expensive to feed them and keep them cool.

Many questions remain, especially why each of the other creatures interdicted by the Bible—vultures, hawks, snakes, snails, shellfish, fish without scales, and so forth—came under the same divine taboo. And why Jews and Moslems, no longer living in the Middle East, continue—with varying degrees of exactitude and zeal—to observe the ancient dietary laws. In general, it appears to me that most of the interdicted birds and animals fall squarely into one of two categories. Some, like ospreys, vultures, and hawks, are not even potentially significant sources of food. Other, like shellfish, are obviously unavailable to mixed pastoral-farming populations. Neither of these categories of tabooed creatures raises the kind of question I have set out to answer—namely, how to account for an apparently bizarre and wasteful taboo. There is obviously nothing irrational about not spending one's time chasing vultures for dinner, or not hiking fifty miles across the desert for a plate of clams on the half shell.

This is an appropriate moment to deny the claim that all religiously sanctioned food practices have ecological explanations. Taboos also have social functions, such as helping people to think of themselves as a distinctive community. This function is well served by the modern observance of dietary rules among Moslems and Jews outside of their Middle Eastern homelands. The question to be put to these practices is whether they diminish in some significant degree the practical and mundane welfare of Jews and Moslems by depriving them of nutritional factors for which there are no readily available substitutes. I think the answer is almost certainly negative. But now permit me to resist another kind of temptation—the temptation to explain everything. I think more will be learned about pig haters if we turn to the other half of the riddle, to the pig lovers.

Pig love is the soulful opposite of the divine opprobrium

that Moslems and Jews heap upon swine. This condition is
not reached through mere gustatory enthusiasm for pork
cookery. Many culinary traditions, including the Euro-American and Chinese, esteem the flesh and fat of pigs. Pig love
is something else. It is a state of total community between
man and pig. While the presence of pigs threatens the human
status of Moslems and Jews, in the ambience of pig love one
cannot truly be human except in the company of pigs.

Pig love includes raising pigs to be a member of the family,
sleeping next to them, talking to them, stroking and fondling
them, calling them by name, leading them on a leash to the
fields, weeping when they fall sick or are injured, and feeding
them with choice morsels from the family table. But unlike
Hindu love of cow, pig love also includes obligatory sacrific-
ing and eating of pigs on special occasions. Because of ritual
slaughter and sacred feasting, pig love provides a broader
prospect for communion between man and beast than is true
of the Hindu farmer and his cow. The climax of pig love is
the incorporation of the pig as flesh into the flesh of the
human host and of the pig as spirit into the spirit of the
ancestors.

Pig love is honoring your dead father by clubbing a beloved
sow to death on his grave site and roasting it in an earth
oven dug on the spot. Pig love is stuffing fistfuls of cold,
salted belly fat into your brother-in-law's mouth to make him
loyal and happy. Above all, pig love is the great pig feast,
held once or twice a generation, when to satisfy the ancestors'
craving for pork, assure communal health, and secure victory
in future wars, most of the adult pigs are killed off and glut-
tonously devoured.

Professor Roy Rappaport of the University of Michigan has

made a detailed study of the relationship between pigs and the pig-loving Maring, a remote group of tribesmen living in the Bismarck Mountains of New Guinea. In his book *Pigs for the Ancestors: Ritual in the Ecology of a New Guinea People*, Rappaport describes how pig love contributes to the solution of basic human problems. Under the given circumstances of Maring life, there are few viable alternatives.

Each local Maring subgroup or clan holds a pig festival on the average about once every twelve years. The entire festival —including various preparations, small-scale sacrifices, and the final massive slaughter—lasts about a year and is known in the Maring language as a *kaiko*. In the first two or three months immediately following the completion of its *kaiko*, the clan engages in armed combat with enemy clans, leading to many casualties and eventual loss or gain of territory. Additional pigs are sacrificed during the fighting, and both the victors and the vanquished soon find themselves entirely bereft of adult pigs with which to curry favor from their respective ancestors. Fighting ceases abruptly, and the belligerents repair to sacred spots to plant small trees known as *rumbim*. Every adult male clansman participates in this ritual by laying hands on the *rumbim* sapling as it is put into the ground.

The war magician addresses the ancestors, explaining that they have run out of pigs and are thankful to be alive. He assures the ancestors that the fighting is now over and that there will be no resumption of hostilities as long as the *rumbim* remains in the ground. From now on, the thoughts and efforts of the living will be directed toward raising pigs; only when a new herd of pigs has been raised, enough for a mighty *kaiko* with which to thank the ancestors properly, will the warriors think of uprooting the *rumbim* and returning to the battlefield.

By a detailed study of one clan called the Tsembaga, Rappaport has been able to show that the entire cycle—which consists of *kaiko*, followed by warfare, the planting of *rumbim*, truce, the raising of a new pig herd, the uprooting of *rumbim*, and new *kaiko*—is no mere psychodrama of pig farmers gone berserk. Every part of this cycle is integrated within a complex, self-regulating ecosystem, that effectively adjusts the size and distribution of the Tsembaga's human and animal population to conform to available resources and production opportunities.

The one question that is central to the understanding of pig love among the Maring is: How do the people decide when they have enough pigs to thank the ancestors properly? The Maring themselves were unable to state how many years should elapse or how many pigs are needed to stage a proper *kaiko*. Possibility of agreement on the basis of a fixed number of animals or years is virtually eliminated because the Maring have no calendar and their language lacks words for numbers larger than three.

The *kaiko* of 1963 observed by Rappaport began when there were 169 pigs and about 200 members of the Tsembaga clan. It is the meaning of these numbers in terms of daily work routines and settlement patterns that provides the key to the length of the cycle.

The task of raising pigs, as well as that of cultivating yams, taro, and sweet potatoes, depends primarily upon the labor of the Maring women. Baby pigs are carried along with human infants to the gardens. After they are weaned, their mistresses train them to trot along behind like dogs. At the age of four or five months, the pigs are turned loose in the forest to scrounge for themselves until their mistresses call them home at night to be fed a daily ration of leftover or substandard sweet potatoes and yams. As each woman's pigs mature and as their numbers increase, she must work harder to provide them with their evening meal.

While the *rumbim* remained in the ground, Rappaport found that the Tsembaga women were under considerable pressure to increase the size of their gardens, to plant more sweet potatoes and yams, and to raise more pigs as quickly as possible in order to have "enough" pigs to hold the next *kaiko* before the enemy did. Mature pigs, weighing about 135 pounds, are heavier than the average adult Maring, and even with their daily scrounging, they cost each woman about as much effort to feed as an adult human. At the time of the uprooting of the *rumbim* in 1963, the more ambitious Tsembaga women were taking care of the equivalent of six 135-pounders in addition to gardening for themselves and their families, cooking, nursing, carrying infants about, and manufacturing household items such as net bags, string aprons, and loincloths. Rappaport calculates that taking care of six pigs alone uses up over 50 percent of the total daily energy which a healthy, well-fed Maring woman is capable of expending.

The increase in the pig population is normally also accompanied by an increase in the human population, especially among groups that have been victorious in the previous war. Pigs and people must be fed from the gardens which are hacked and burned out of the tropical forest that covers the slopes of the Bismarck Mountains. Like similar horticultural systems in other tropical areas, the fertility of the Maring

49

gardens depends upon the nitrogen that is put into the soil by the ashes left from burning off the trees. These gardens cannot be planted for more than two or three years consecutively, since once the trees are gone, the heavy rains quickly wash away the nitrogen and other soil nutrients. The only remedy is to choose another site and burn off another segment of the forest. After a decade or so, the old gardens get covered over with enough secondary growth so that they can be burned again and replanted. These old garden sites are preferred because they are easier to clear than virgin forest. But as the pig and human populations spurt upward during the *rumbim* truce, the maturation of the old garden sites lags behind and new gardens must be established in the virgin tracts. While there is plenty of virgin forest available, the new garden sites place an extra strain on everybody and lower the typical rate of return for every unit of labor the Maring invest in feeding themselves and their pigs.

The men whose task it is to clear and burn the new gardens must work harder because of the greater thickness and height of the virgin trees. But it is the women who suffer most, since the new gardens are necessarily located at a greater distance from the center of the village. Not only must the women plant larger gardens to feed their families and pigs, but they must consume more and more of their time just walking to work and more and more of their energy hauling piglets and babies up to and down from the garden and the heavy loads of harvested yams and sweet potatoes back to their houses.

A further source of tension arises from the increased effort involved in protecting the gardens from being eaten up by the mature pigs that are let loose to scrounge for themselves. Every garden must be surrounded by a stout fence to keep the pigs out. A hungry 150-pound sow, however, is a formidable adversary. Fences are breached and gardens invaded more frequently as the pig herd multiplies. If caught by an irate gardener, the offending pig may be killed. These disagreeable incidents set neighbor against neighbor and heighten the general sense of dissatisfaction. As Rappaport points out, incidents involving pigs necessarily increase more rapidly than the pigs themselves.

In order to avoid such incidents and to get closer to their gardens, the Maring begin to move their houses farther apart over a wider area. This dispersion lowers the security of the group in case of renewed hostilities. So everyone becomes more jittery. The women begin to complain about being overworked. They bicker with their husbands and snap at their children. Soon the men begin to wonder if perhaps there are "enough pigs." They go down to inspect the *rumbim* to see how tall it has grown. The women complain more loudly, and finally the men, with considerable unanimity and without counting the pigs, agree that the moment has come to begin the *kaiko*.

During the *kaiko* year of 1963, the Tsembaga killed off three-fourths of their pigs by number and seven-eighths by weight. Much of this meat was distributed to in-laws and military allies who were invited to participate in the year-long festivities. At the climactic rituals held on November 7 and 8, 1963, 96 pigs were killed and their meat and fat were distributed directly or indirectly to an estimated two or three thousand people. The Tsembaga kept about 2,500 pounds of pork and fat for themselves, or 12 pounds for each man, woman, and child, a quantity which they consumed in five consecutive days of unrestrained gluttony.

The Maring consciously use the *kaiko* as an occasion to reward their allies for previous assistance and to seek their loyalty in future hostilities. The allies in turn accept the invitation to the *kaiko* because it gives them an opportunity to decide if their hosts are prosperous and powerful enough to warrant continued support; of course, the allies are also hungry for pig meat.

Guests dress up in their finest manner. They wear bead-and-shell necklaces, cowrie-shell garters around their calves, orchid-fiber waistbands, purple-striped loincloths bordered with marsupial fur, and masses of accordion-shaped leaves topped by a bustle on their buttocks. Crowns of eagle and parrot feathers encircle their heads, festooned with orchid stems, green beetles and cowries, and topped with an entire stuffed bird of paradise. Every man has spent hours painting his face in some original design, and wears his best bird-of-paradise plume through his nose along with a favorite disk or a gold-lip crescent shell. Visitors and hosts spend much time showing off to each other by dancing at the specially constructed dance ground, preparing the way for amorous alliances with the female onlookers as well as military alliances with male warriors.

Over a thousand people crowded into the Tsembaga dance ground to participate in the rituals that followed the great pig slaughter witnessed by Rappaport in 1963. Special reward packages of salted pig fat were heaped high behind the window of a three-sided ceremonial building that adjoined the dance grounds. In Rappaport's words:

Several men climbed to the top of the structure and from there proclaimed one by one to the multitude the names and clans of the men being honored. As his name was called, each honored man charged toward the ... window swinging his ax and shouting. His supporters, yelling battle cries, beating drums, brandishing weapons, followed close behind him. At the window the mouth of the honored man was stuffed with cold salted belly-fat by the Tsembaga whom he had come to help in the last fight and who now also passed out to him through the window a package containing additional salted belly for his followers. With the belly fat hanging from his mouth the hero now retired, his supporters close behind him, shouting, singing, beating their drums, dancing. Honored name quickly followed honored name, and groups charging toward the window sometimes became entangled with those retiring.

Within limits set by the basic technological and environmental conditions of the Maring, all of this has a practical explanation. First of all, the craving for pig meat is a perfectly rational feature of Maring life in view of the general scarcity of meat in their diet. While they can supplement their staple vegetables with occasional frogs, rats, and a few hunted marsupials, domesticated pork is their best potential source of high-quality animal fat and protein. This does not mean that the Maring suffer from an acute form of protein deficiency. On the contrary, their diet of yams, sweet potatoes, taro, and other plant foods provides them with a broad variety of vegetable proteins that satisfies but does not far exceed minimum nutritional standards. Getting proteins from pigs is something else, however. Animal protein in general is more concentrated and metabolically more effective than vegetable protein, so for human populations that are mainly restricted to vegetable foods (no cheese, milk, eggs, or fish), meat is always an irresistible temptation.

Moreover, up to a point, it makes good ecological sense for

the Maring to raise pigs. The temperature and humidity are ideal. Pigs thrive in the damp, shady environment of the mountain slopes and obtain a substantial portion of their food by roaming freely over the forest floor. The complete interdiction of pork—the Middle Eastern solution—would be a most irrational and uneconomic practice under these conditions.

On the other hand, unlimited growth of the pig population can only lead to competition between man and pig. If permitted to go too far, pig farming overburdens the women and endangers the gardens upon which the Maring depend for survival. As the pig population increases, the Maring women must work harder and harder. Eventually they find themselves working to feed pigs rather than to feed people. As virgin lands are brought into use, the efficiency of the entire agricultural system plummets. It is at this point that the *kaiko* takes place, the role of the ancestors being to encourage a maximum effort at pig raising but at the same time to see to it that the pigs do not destroy the women and the gardens. Their task is admittedly more difficult than Jahweh's or Allah's, since a total taboo is always easier to administer than a partial one. Nonetheless, the belief that a *kaiko* must be held as soon as possible, in order to keep the ancestors happy, effectively rids the Maring of animals that have grown parasitic and helps keep the pig population from becoming "too much of a good thing."

If the ancestors are so clever, why don't they simply set a limit on the number of pigs that each Maring woman can raise? Would it not be better to keep a constant number of pigs than to permit the pig population to cycle through extremes of scarcity and abundance?

54

This alternative would be preferable only if each Maring clan had zero population growth, no enemies, a wholly different form of agriculture, powerful rulers, and written laws —in short, if they weren't the Maring. No one, not even the ancestors, can predict how many pigs are "too much of a good thing." The point at which the pigs become burdensome does not depend upon any set of constants, but rather on a set of variables which changes from year to year. It depends on how many people there are in the whole region and in each clan, on their state of physical and psychological vigor, on the size of their territory, on the amount of secondary forest they have, and on the condition and intentions of the enemy groups in neighboring territories. The Tsembaga's ancestors cannot simply say "thou shalt keep four pigs, and no more," because there is no way of guaranteeing that the ancestors of the Kundugai, Dimbagai, Yimgagai, Tuguma, Aundagai, Kauwasi, Monambant, and all the rest will agree to this number. All of these groups are engaged in a struggle to validate their respective claims to a share in the earth's resources. Warfare and the threat of warfare probe and test these claims. The ancestors' insatiable craving for pigs is a consequence of this armed probing and testing by the Maring clans.

To satisfy the ancestors, a maximum effort must be made not only to produce as much food as possible, but to accumulate it in the form of the pig herd. This effort, even though it results in cyclical surpluses of pork, enhances the ability of the group to survive and to defend its territory.

It does this in several ways. First, the extra effort called forth by the pig lust of the ancestors raises the levels of protein intake for the entire group during the *rumbim* truce, resulting in a taller, healthier, and more vigorous population. Furthermore, by linking the *kaiko* to the end of the truce, the ancestors guarantee that massive doses of high-quality fats and proteins are consumed at the period of greatest social stress—in the months immediately prior to the outbreak of intergroup fighting. Finally, by banking large amounts of extra food in the form of nutritionally valuable pig meat, the Maring clans are able to attract and reward allies when they are most needed, again just before the outbreak of war.

The Tsembaga and their neighbors are conscious of the relationship between success in raising pigs and military power. The number of pigs slaughtered at the *kaiko* provides the guests with an accurate basis for judging the health, energy, and determination of the feast givers. A group that cannot manage to accumulate pigs is not likely to put up a good defense of its territory, and will not attract strong allies. No mere irrational premonition of defeat hangs over the battlefield when one's ancestors aren't given enough pork at the *kaiko*. Rappaport insists—correctly, I believe—that in a fundamental ecological sense, the size of a group's pig surplus does indicate its productive and military strength and does validate or invalidate its territorial claims. In other words, the entire system results in an efficient distribution of plants, animals, and people in the region, from a human ecological point of view.

I am sure that many readers will now want to insist that the pig love is maladaptive and terribly inefficient because it is geared to periodic outbreaks of warfare. If warfare is irrational, then so is the *kaiko*. Again, permit me to resist the temptation to explain everything at once. In the next chapter

I will discuss the mundane causes of Maring warfare. But for the moment, let me point out that warfare is not caused by pig love. Millions of people who have never even seen a pig wage war; nor does pig hatred (ancient and modern) discernibly enhance the peacefulness of the intergroup relations in the Middle East. Given the prevalence of warfare in human history and prehistory, we can only marvel at the ingenious system devised by New Guinea "savages" for maintaining extensive periods of truce. After all, as long as their neighbor's *rumbim* remains in the ground, the Tsembaga don't have to worry about being attacked. One can perhaps say as much, but not more, about nations that plant missiles instead of *rumbim*.

Primitive War

WARS WAGED by scattered primitive tribes like the Maring raise doubts about the basic sanity of human lifestyles. When modern nation-states go to war we often puzzle over the precise cause, but seldom lack plausible alternative explanations from which to choose.

History books brim with details of wars in which the combatants struggled for mastery over trade routes, natural resources, cheap labor, or mass markets. The wars of modern empires may be lamentable, but they are not inscrutable. This distinction is basic to the present-day nuclear détente, which rests on the assumption that wars involve some sort of rational balance of gains and losses. If the United States and the Soviet Union clearly stand to lose more than they can possibly gain by nuclear attack, neither is likely to initiate a war as the solution to its problems. But this system can be expected to prevent nuclear war only if wars in general are related to practical and mundane conditions. The probability of self-annihilation won't discourage warfare if wars are fought for irrational and inscrutable reasons. If wars are fought, as some believe, primarily because man is "warlike," instinctually "aggressive," an animal who kills for sport, for glory, for vengeance, or for the sheer love of blood and violent excitement, then kiss those missiles goodbye.

Irrational and inscrutable motives predominate in current explanations of primitive warfare. Since war has deadly consequences for its participants, it seems presumptuous to doubt that the combatants know why they are fighting. But cows, pigs, wars, or witches, the answers to our riddles do not lie within the participants' consciousness. The belligerents themselves seldom grasp the systemic causes and consequences of their battles. They tend to explain war by describing the personal feelings and motivations experienced immediately prior to the outbreak of hostilities. A Jívaro about to set off on a headhunting expedition welcomes the opportunity to capture the soul of the enemy; the Crow warrior yearns to touch the dead foeman's body to prove his fearlessness; other warriors are inspired by the thought of vengeance, still others by the prospect of eating human flesh.

These exotic yearnings are real enough, but they are the results rather than the causes of war. They mobilize the human potential for violence and help to organize warlike behavior. Primitive war, like cow love or pig hate, has a practical basis. Primitive peoples go to war because they lack alternative solutions to certain problems—alternative solutions that would involve less suffering and fewer premature deaths.

The Maring, like many other primitive groups, explain their going to war in terms of the need to avenge violent acts. In every instance collected by Rappaport, previously friendly clans began to make war on each other following allegations of specific acts of violence. The most frequently cited provocations were abduction of women, rape, the shooting of a pig in a garden, theft of crops, poaching, and death or disease induced through withcraft.

Once two Maring clans had engaged in warfare in which fatalities had occurred, they never lacked motivation to renew hostilities. Each battlefield death was brooded over by the victim's relatives, who never felt satisfied until they had evened the score by killing one of the enemy. Each round of fighting provided sufficient motivation for the next, and Maring warriors often went into battle with a burning desire to kill specific members of the enemy group—the ones who ten years before had been responsible for killing a father or brother.

I have already told part of the story of how the Maring prepare for war. After uprooting the sacred *rumbim*, belligerent clans hold the great pig festivals at which they attempt to recruit new allies and consolidate relationships with previously friendly groups. The *kaiko* is a noisy affair, various phases of which go on for months, so there is no possibility of launching a sneak attack. In fact, the Maring hope that the opulence of their *kaiko* will demoralize their enemies. Both sides make preparation for battle well in advance of the first encounters. Through intermediaries, an unforested area located in the borderland between the combatants is agreed upon as an appropriate fight ground. Both sides participate, alternately, in clearing this site of underbrush, and fighting begins on an agreed-upon day.

Before leaving for the fight ground, the warriors gather in a circle around their war magicians, who kneel by the fire, sobbing and conversing with the ancestors. The magicians place lengths of green bamboo in the flames. When the heat makes the bamboo explode, the warriors stamp their feet, cry *Ooooooo*, and move to the battlefield in single file, prancing and singing along the way. The opposing forces array themselves at opposite ends of the clearing within bowshot of each other. They plant their man-sized wooden shields in the ground, take cover, and yell threats and insults at the enemy. Occasionally a warrior pops out from behind his shield to taunt his adversaries, darting back as a shower of arrows is loosed in his direction. Casualties are low during this phase of the fighting, and allies in both camps attempt to end the war as soon as someone is seriously injured. If either side insists on further vengeance, the fighting escalates. The warriors bring axes and jabbing spears into play, and the opposing ranks draw closer to each other. Either side may now rush the other in a determined attempt to produce fatalities.

As soon as someone gets killed, there is a truce. For a day or two, all the warriors stay home in order to carry out funerary rituals or praise their ancestors. But if both sides remain evenly matched, they soon return to the fight ground. As the struggle drags on, the allies become weary and are tempted to go home to their own villages. If defections accumulate more in one group than the other, the stronger force may attempt to rush the weaker and chase them from the field. The weaker clan gathers up its movable possessions and flees to its allies' villages. The stronger clans, anticipating victory, may seek to press the advantage by sweeping down on the enemy village at night, setting fire to it and killing as many people as they can find.

Primitive War

When a rout takes place, the victors do not pursue the enemy but concentrate instead upon killing stragglers, burning buildings, destroying crops, and abducting pigs. Nineteen of twenty-nine known wars among the Maring ended in one group routing another. Immediately after a rout, the victorious group returns to its village, sacrifices its remaining pigs, and plants the new *rumbim,* initiating the period of the truce. It does not directly occupy the enemy's lands.

A decisive rout in which many people are killed may lead a group never to return to its former territory. The losers' descent lines merge with those of their allies and hosts, while their territory is taken over by the victors and the victors' allies. Occasionally, the defeated group cedes its boundary lands to the allies among whom it has sought refuge. Professor Andrew Vayda, who has studied the aftermath of wars in the Bismarck Range region, says that whether a defeated group had been decisively routed or not, it is likely to establish its new settlement farther away from the enemy borders.

Much interest centers on the question of whether the fighting and territorial adjustments among the Maring results from what is loosely called "population pressure." If by "population pressure" we mean the absolute inability of a group to meet minimum calorie requirements, then we cannot say that there is population pressure in the Maring region. When the Tsembaga held their pig festival in 1963, the human population stood at 200 and the pig population at 169. Rappaport calculates that the Tsembaga had enough unused forest lands in their territory to feed an additional 84 people (or 84 mature pigs) without producing any permanent damage to the forest cover or degrading other vital aspects to their habitat. But I object to defining population pressure as the onset of actual nutritional deficiencies or the actual beginning of irreversible damage to the environment. In my opinion, population pressure exists as soon as a population begins to move closer to the point of calorie or protein deficiencies, or as soon as it begins to grow and consume at a rate which sooner or later must degrade and deplete the life-sustaining capacities of its environment.

The population size at which nutritional deficiencies and degradation begin to occur is the upper limit of what ecologists call the habitat's "carrying capacity." Like the Maring, most primitive societies possess institutional mechanisms for restricting and reversing population growth well below carrying capacity. This discovery has led to much befuddlement. Since particular human groups cut back on population, production, and consumption in advance of any discernibly negative consequences caused by overshooting carrying capacity, some experts claim that population pressure cannot be the cause of the cutbacks. But we do not have to see a safety valve get stuck and a boiler explode in order to judge that the valve is there because it normally prevents the boiler from destroying itself.

There is no great mystery either about how these cutoffs —the cultural equivalents of thermostats, safety valves, and circuit breakers—became part of tribal life. As in the case of other adaptive evolutionary novelties, groups that invented or adopted growth cutoff institutions survived more consistently than those that blundered forward across the limit of carrying capacity. Primitive warfare is neither capricious nor instinctive; it is simply one of the cutoff mechanisms that help to keep human populations in a state of ecological equilibrium with respect to their habitats.

Primitive War

Most of us prefer to regard warfare not as a safeguard but as a threat to sound ecological relationships brought on by irrepressible and irrational behavior. Many of my friends think it is sinful to say that war is a rational solution to any kind of problem. Yet I think that my explanation of primitive warfare as an ecological adaptation provides more grounds for optimism about the prospects for ending modern warfare than currently popular aggressive instinct theories. As I said earlier, if wars are caused by innate human killer instincts, there is not much we can do about preventing them. If, on the other hand, wars are caused by practical conditions and relationships, then we can reduce the threat of warfare by changing those conditions and relationships.

I don't want to be labeled an advocate of war, so permit me to make the following disclaimer: I am saying that warfare is an ecologically adaptive lifestyle among primitive peoples, *not* that modern wars are ecologically adaptive. With nuclear weapons, war can now be escalated to the point of total mutual annihilation. So we have arrived at a phase in the evolution of our species when the next great adaptive advance must either be the elimination of nuclear weapons or the elimination of war itself.

The system-regulating or system-maintaining functions of Maring warfare can be inferred from several different lines of evidence. First of all, we know that warfare breaks out at a point where production and consumption are booming and the pig and human populations are building back up from the lows reached at the end of the previous fight. The cutoff pig festival and subsequent hostilities don't coincide with the same maxima for every cycle. Some clan groups try to validate their land claims at levels below previous maxima as a result of the disproportionately rapid build-up of enemy neighbors. Others may delay their pig festival until they actually transgress the threshold of the carrying capacity of their local territory. The important thing, however, is not the regulating effects of warfare upon the population of one or another clan, but upon the population of the Maring region as a whole.

Primitive warfare does not achieve its regulating effects primarily through deaths in combat. Even among nations that practice industrialized forms of killing, combat deaths do not substantially affect the rate of population growth. Tens of millions of battle fatalities in the twentieth century show up as a slight hesitation in the growth curve's implacable upward thrust. Take the case of Russia: During the height of the fighting and famine of World War I and the Bolshevik revolution, the correlation between projected peacetime population and actual wartime population was off by only a few percentage points. One decade after the fighting had ceased, the Russian population had fully recuperated and was right back on the curve where it would have been if the war and the revolution had never occurred. Another example: in Vietnam, despite the extraordinary intensity of the ground and air wars, population rose steadily all through the 1960's.

Referring to catastrophes like World War II, Frank Livingstone of the University of Michigan has said quite bluntly: "When we consider that these slaughters only occur about once in a generation, the conclusion seems inescapable that they have no effect on the population growth or size." One reason for this is that the average woman is extremely fecund and can easily give birth eight or nine times during the twenty-five to thirty-five years during which she can bear children. In World War II, the number of all war-induced deaths remained below 10 percent of the population, and a slight increase in the number of births per woman could easily have made up the deficit in a few years. (There was also an assist from a lowering of infant mortality rates and a lowering of the death rate in general.)

I can't tell you the actual rates of war deaths among the Maring. But among the Yanomamo, a tribe that is located on the border between Brazil and Venezuela and is reputed to be one of the world's most warlike primitive groups, about 15 percent of the adults die as a result of warfare. I shall have a great deal more to say about the Yanomamo in the next chapter.

The most important reason for downgrading combat as a means of population control is that everywhere in the world, males are the main belligerents and the principal victims of battlefield engagements. Among the Yanomamo, for example, only 7 percent of adult women versus 33 percent of adult men die in battle. According to Andrew Vayda, the bloodiest rout among the Maring resulted in fatalities for fourteen men, six women, and three children out of a population of three hundred in the defeated clan. Male combat deaths can be dismissed as being virtually without effect on the reproductive potential of groups like the Tsembaga. Even if 75 percent of the adult males were killed off in one big battle, the surviving females could easily make up the deficit in a single generation.

Like most primitive societies, the Maring and Yanomamo are polygynous, meaning that many men have several wives. All women get married as soon as they can bear children and remain married throughout their entire reproductive life span. Any normal human male can keep four or five fertile women pregnant most of the time. When a Maring man dies, there are plenty of brothers and nephews waiting to add the widow to their ménage. Even from a subsistence point of view, most males are entirely dispensable, and their deaths in combat need create no insurmountable difficulties for their widows and children. Among the Maring, as I mentioned in the previous chapter, the women are the main gardeners and pig raisers anyway. This is true of cut-and-burn subsistence systems all over the world. The men contribute to the gardening by burning off the forest cover, but women are perfectly capable of carrying out this heavy work on their own. In most primitive societies, whenever there are heavy loads to be moved—firewood or baskets of yams—the women, not the men, are regarded as the appropriate "beasts of burden." Given the minimal contribution which Maring males make to subsistence, the higher the percentage of women in the population, the higher the overall efficiency of food production. As far as food is concerned, the Maring men are like the pigs: They consume much more than they produce. The women and children would eat better if they concentrated on raising pigs instead of men.

So the adaptive significance of Maring warfare cannot consist of the brute effect of combat deaths upon population growth. Instead, I think that warfare preserves the Maring ecosystem through two rather indirect and less-known consequences. One of these has to do with the fact that as a result of warfare, local groups are forced to abandon their prime garden areas at a point below carrying capacity. The

other is that warfare increases the rate of female infant
mortality, and thus despite the demographic insignificance
of male combat deaths, warfare acts as an effective regulator
of regional population growth.

First, let me explain the abandonment of prime garden
lands. For several years after a rout, neither victors nor vanquished use the defeated group's central gardening area,
which consists of the best, middle-altitude, secondary forest
sites. This abandonment, although temporary, helps to maintain the carrying capacity of the region. When the Kundegai
defeated the Tsembaga in 1953, they tore up the Tsembaga
gardens, destroyed groves of fruit trees, desecrated the burial
grounds and pig ovens, burned the houses, slaughtered all
the adult pigs they could find, and carried off all the baby
pigs to their villages. As Rappaport says, the depradations
were directed toward making it difficult for the Tsembaga
to return to their own territory, rather than toward the
acquisition of booty. The Kundegai, fearing the vengeance
of the Tsembaga's ancestor ghosts, withdrew to their own
territory. There they hung up certain magic fight stones in
net bags inside a sacred shelter. These stones were not taken
down until the Kundegai were able to thank their own ancestors at the next pig festival. As long as the stones remained
up, the Kundegai were fearful of the ancestral spirits of the
Tsembaga and refrained from gardening or hunting on
Tsembaga territory. As it happened, the Tsembaga themselves eventually reoccupied the abandoned lands. In other
wars, as I have said, the victors or their allies eventually
made use of the lands left temporarily vacant by routs. But
in any event, the immediate effect of a rout is that intensively

cultivated portions of forest are placed in fallow while previously unused areas—the border areas of the loser's territory—are placed under cultivation.

In the New Guinea highlands, as well as in all other tropical forest regions, repeated burning and cutting of the same area threatens the forest's recuperative powers. If the interval between successive burnings is too short, the soil becomes dry and hard and the trees cannot reseed themselves. Grasses invade the garden sites, and the entire habitat gradually changes from rich primary forest to gullied and eroded grasslands that cannot be used for traditional kinds of agriculture. Millions of acres of grasslands throughout the world are known to have been produced by this sequence.

Among the Maring, relatively little deforestation has occurred. There are some patches of permanent grassland and degraded secondary forest in the territory of large and aggressive groups such as the Kundegai—the group that was responsible for the rout of the Tsembaga in 1953. But the life-destroying consequence of trying to force the forest to sustain more pigs and people than it can tolerate are evident in many nearby regions of the New Guinea highlands. For example, a recent study of the South Foré region by Dr. Arthur Sorenson of the National Institutes of Health shows that the Foré have inflicted large-scale irreversible damage upon their primary forest habitat over a four-hundred-square-mile area of the Central Range. Thick Kunai grass has taken the place of abandoned garden and hamlet sites, following the movement of settlement deeper into the virgin forests. A general breaking up of the forest can be seen in regions where gardening has been carried out for many years. I think that the Maring's ritually timed cycle of war, *rumbim* peace, and pig slaughter has helped to protect the Maring habitat from a similar fate.

Amid all the bizarre events that take place during the ritual cycle—the *rumbim* planting, pig slaughter, the hanging of the magic fight stones, and the war itself—a simple matter of timing strikes me as more amazing than anything else. In the Maring region, gardens must lie fallow for a minimum of ten to twelve consecutive years before they can be burned and replanted without danger of being degraded into grassland. The pig festivals also occur about twice a generation—or every ten to twelve years. This can't be a mere coincidence. So I think we can now at last answer the question "When do the Maring have enough pigs to thank the ancestors?" Answer: "They have enough pigs when the forest has grown back over the routed group's former garden area."

The Maring, like other cut-and-burn people, live by "eating the forest"—burning trees and planting crops in the ashes. Their ritual cycle and ceremonialized war prevents them from eating too much forest too fast. The routed group draws back from the lands topographically best suited for gardens. This permits regeneration of forest cover in endangered sectors where they and their pigs have eaten too much. During the sojourn among their allies, the people who have been routed may return to make use of portions of their territory, but at unendangered sites in primary forest remote from their enemies. If they succeed, with the help of their allies, in raising many pigs and building back their strength, they will attempt to reoccupy their lands and place them into full production once again. The rhythm of war and peace, strength and weakness, many pigs and few pigs, central gardens and peripheral gardens, evokes corresponding pulses in all the neighboring clans. Although the victors do not immediately seek to occupy their enemy's territory, they plant gardens closer to the routed enemy's border than they did before the war. Most importantly, their pig population has been drastically reduced, yielding at least a temporary cutback in the rate of advance toward the threshold of the territory's carrying capacity. When the pig population approaches maximum, the victors take down the magic fight stones, uproot the *rumbim,* and prepare to enter the unoccupied and newly regenerated territory— peacefully if their former enemies are still too weak to engage them, vengefully if their former enemies have moved back.

In the linked pulsations of people, pigs, gardens, and forests we can well understand why the pigs acquire a ritual sanctity regarded as incompatible with swinedom in other parts of the world. Since one adult pig eats as much forest as one adult human, pig slaughter reduces man slaughter at the climax of each successive pulse. No wonder the ancestors crave pigs; otherwise they would have to "eat" their sons and daughters!

One problem remains. When the Tsembaga were routed from their territory in 1953, they sought refuge with seven different local groups. In some cases, the clans they went to live with took in additional "refugees" from other wars before and after the defeat of the Tsembaga. It would seem, therefore, that the ecological threat to the routed groups' territories had merely been transferred from one place to another, and that the refugees would soon begin to eat up their hosts' forests. So mere displacement of people is not sufficient to keep the population from degrading the environment. There must also be some way of limiting actual population growth. This brings us to the second consequence of primitive warfare which I mentioned a moment ago.

In most primitive societies, warfare is an effective means of population control because intense, recurring intergroup combat places a premium upon rearing male rather than female infants. The more numerous the adult males, the stronger the military force which a group dependent upon hand weapons can put into the field and the more likely it is to hold onto its territory against the pressure exerted by its neighbors. According to a demographic survey of over 600 primitive populations carried out by William T. Divale of the American Museum of Natural History, there is an extraordinary consistent imbalance of boys over girls in the junior and infant age ranks (up to about 15 years old). The average ratio of boys to girls is 150:100, but some groups even have twice as many boys as girls. The Tsembaga ratio of boys to girls falls close to the average of 150:100. When we turn to the adult age ranks, however, the average ratio between men and women in Divale's study falls closer to unity, suggesting a higher death rate for mature males than mature females.

Combat casualties are the most likely reason for the higher death rate among adult males. Among the Maring, male battle casualties outnumber female casualties by as much as 10 to 1. But what accounts for the reverse situation in the junior and infant age categories?

Divale's answer is that many primitive groups follow a practice of overt female infanticide. Female children are suffocated or simply left unattended in the bush. But more often infanticide is covert, and people usually deny that they practice it—just as the Hindu farmers deny that they kill their cows. Like the unbalanced sex ratio among cattle in India, the discrepancy between human female and male infant mortality rates usually results from a neglectful pattern of infant care, rather than from any direct assault on the female baby's life. Even a slight difference in a mother's responsiveness to her children's cries for food or protection might cumulatively account for the entire imbalance in the human sex ratios.

Only an extremely powerful set of cultural forces can explain the practice of female infanticide and the preferential treatment given to male infants. In strictly biological terms, females are more valuable than males. Most males are reproductively redundant, since one man can suffice to impregnate hundreds of females. Only females can give birth to the young and only females can nurse them (in societies that lack baby bottles and formula substitutes for mother's milk). If there is going to be any kind of sex discrimination against infants, one would predict that the males would be the victims. But it is the other way around. This paradox gets harder to understand if we admit that women are physically and mentally capable of performing all the basic tasks of production and subsistence quite independently of any help from males. Women can do every job that men can do, although perhaps with some loss of efficiency where brute strength is required. They can hunt with bows and arrows, fish, set traps, and cut down trees if taught to do so or permitted to learn. They can and do carry heavy burdens, and they can and do work in gardens and fields throughout the world. Among cut-and-burn horticulturalists like the Maring, women are the main food producers. Even among hunting groups like the Bushmen, female labor provides over two-thirds of the group's nutritional needs. As for the inconveniences associated with menstruation and pregnancy, modern leaders of women's liberation are quite correct when they point out that these "problems" can easily be eliminated in most jobs and production activities by minor changes in work schedules. The alleged biological basis for a sexual division of labor is a lot of nonsense. As long as all the females in a group are not found in the same stage of pregnancy at the same time, the economic functions considered to be the natural male prerogative—like hunting or herding—could be managed very nicely by women alone.

The one human activity, other than sex itself, for which male specialization is indispensable is armed conflict involving hand weapons. On the average, men are taller, heavier, and more muscular than women. Men can throw a longer spear, bend a stronger bow, and use a bigger club. Men can also run faster—toward an enemy in attack and away from one in defeat. To insist along with some women's liberation leaders that women too can be trained to fight with hand weapons does not alter the picture. If any primitive group ever trained women rather than men as its military specialists, it made a big mistake. Such a group surely committed suicide because not a single authentic case is known from any quarter of the globe.

Warfare inverts the relative value of the contribution made by males and females to a group's prospects for survival. By placing a premium upon maximizing the number of combat-ready adult males, warfare obliges primitive societies to limit their nurturance of females. It is this, and

77

not combat per se, that makes warfare an effective means of controlling population growth. As every Maring knows, the ancestors help those who most help themselves by putting lots of men on the fight ground and keeping them there. So I am rather inclined to the view that the entire ritual cycle is a clever "trick" on the part of the ancestors to get the Maring to breed pigs and men instead of women, in order to protect the forest.

In further pursuit of the practical conditions that lead to primitive warfare, I still have to confront the question of why less violent means for keeping the local group's population below carrying capacity weren't used. For example, would it not have served the Tsembaga better and their habitat equally well had they simply limited their population through some technique of birth control? The answer is no, because prior to the invention of the condom in the eighteenth century there were no safe, relatively pleasurable, and effective contraceptive devices in use anywhere. Previously, the most effective "peaceful" means for limiting population, other than infanticide, was abortion. Many primitive peoples know how to induce abortion by drinking poisonous concoctions. Others instruct the pregnant mother to wrap a tight band of cloth around her belly. When all else fails, the pregnant woman lies on her back while a friend jumps full force onto her abdomen. These methods are fairly effective, but they have the unpleasant side effect of killing the mother-to-be only slightly less often than they kill the embryo.

Lacking any safe and effective means of contraception or abortion, primitive peoples must focus their institutionalized means of population control on individuals who are already alive. Children are the logical victims of these efforts—the younger the better—since number one, they can't resist; number two, there is less of a social and material investment in them; and number three, the emotional ties to infants are easier to cut than those between adults.

Anyone who finds my reasoning depraved or "uncivilized" should read about eighteenth-century England. Gin-soaked mothers by the tens of thousands regularly dropped their babies into the Thames or wrapped them in the clothing of smallpox victims, left them in trash barrels, rolled over on top of them during drunken stupors, and otherwise contrived to shorten their babies' lives by direct or indirect means. In our own times, only an incredible degree of self-righteous pigheadedness prevents us from admitting that infanticide is still being practiced on a cosmic scale in the underdeveloped nations, where first-year infant mortality rates of 250 per 1,000 births are commonplace.

The Maring make the best of a bad situation—the universal plight of mankind before the development of effective contraception and safe early-term abortion. They induce or tolerate a higher proportion of female infant deaths than male infant deaths. If there were no discrimination against female babies, many male babies would fall victim to the need for population control. War, which places a premium upon the rearing of the maximum number of males, is responsible for the higher survival rate of male as compared with female infants. Or to sum it all up, war is the price that primitive societies pay for raising sons when they cannot afford to rear daughters.

The study of primitive war leads to the conclusion that war has been part of an adaptive strategy associated with particular technological, demographic, and ecological conditions. We need not invoke imaginary killer instincts or inscrutable or capricious motives to understand why armed combat has been so common in human history. This being the case, we have every reason to hope that when humanity stands to lose more than it can possibly gain from war, other means of resolving intergroup conflicts will take its place.

The Savage Male

FEMALE INFANTICIDE is one manifestation of male supremacy. I think it can be shown that other manifestations of male supremacy are also rooted in the practical exigencies of armed conflict.

To explain human sexual hierarchies we must again choose between theories that stress unmodifiable instincts and theories which emphasize the adaptiveness of lifestyles with respect to modifiable practical and mundane conditions. I am inclined to the women's liberationist view that "anatomy is not destiny," by which it is meant that innate sexual differences cannot account for the unequal distribution of privileges and powers between men and women within the domestic, economic, and political spheres. Women's liberationists do not deny that the possession of ovaries rather than testicles necessarily leads to different kinds of life experiences. What they deny is that there is something in the biological nature of men and women that by itself destines human males to enjoy greater sexual, economic, and political privileges than females.

Apart from childbearing and related sexual specialties, the assignment of social roles on the basis of sex does not follow automatically from the biological differences between men and women. Knowing only the facts of human anatomy and biology, one could not predict that females would be the socially subordinate sex. This is because the human species is unique in the animal kingdom for the lack of correspondence between its hereditary anatomical equipment and its means of subsistence and defense. We are the world's most dangerous species not because we have the biggest teeth, sharpest claws, most venomous sting, or thickest skin, but because we know how to equip ourselves with deadly tools and weapons that perform the functions of teeth, claws, stings, and hides more effectively than any mere anatomical device. Our primary mode of biological adaptation is culture, not anatomy. I no more expect men to dominate women simply because they are taller and heavier, than I expect the human species to be ruled over by cattle or horses—animals that outweigh the average husband by an amount thirty times greater than he outweighs his wife. In human societies, sexual dominance is not settled by which sex is bigger or innately more assertive, but rather by which sex controls the technology of defense and aggression.

If I had knowledge only of the anatomy and cultural capacities of men and women, I would predict that women rather than men would be more likely to gain control over the technology of defense and aggression, and that if one sex were going to subordinate the other, it would be female over male. While I would be impressed with the physical dimorphism—the greater height, weight, and strength of the males—especially in relationship to hand-held weapons, I would be even more impressed by something which the females have and which the males cannot get—namely, control over the birth, care, and feeding of babies. Women, in other words, control the nursery, and because they control the nursery, they can potentially modify any lifestyle that threatens them. It is within their power of selective neglect to produce a sex ratio heavily in favor of females over males. It also lies within woman's power to sabotage the development of "masculine" males by rewarding little boys for being passive rather than aggressive. I would expect women to concentrate their efforts on rearing solidary and aggressive females rather than males. I would further expect the few male survivors per generation to be shy, obedient, hardworking, and grateful for sexual favors. I would predict that women would monopolize the headship of local groups, that they would be responsible for shamanistic relations with the supernatural, and that God would be called SHE. Finally, I would expect that the ideal and most prestigious form of marriage would be polyandry—one woman controlling the sexual and economic services of several men.

Female-dominated social systems of this type were actually postulated as the primordial condition of mankind by various theoreticians who lived in the nineteenth century. Friedrich Engels, for example, who got his ideas from the American anthropologist Lewis Henry Morgan, believed that modern societies had passed through a matriarchal phase during which descent was reckoned exclusively in the female line and women were politically dominant over men. Many modern-day women's liberationists continue to believe in this myth and its sequel. Supposedly, the subordinate males banned together and overthrew the matriarchs, took away their weapons, and have been conspiring ever since to exploit and degrade the female sex. Some women who accept this kind of analysis argue that the balance between male and female power and authority can be righted only by a militant counterconspiracy equivalent to a kind of guerrilla war between the sexes.

There is one thing wrong with this theory: No one has ever been able to authenticate a single case that is representative of true matriarchy. The only evidence for such a phase, aside from ancient myths about Amazons, is that about 10 to 15 percent of the world's societies trace kinship and descent exclusively through females. But the tracing of descent through females is matrilineality, not matriarchy. While the position of women in matrilineal kin groups tends to be relatively good, the principal features of matriarchy are absent. Males rather than females dominate economic, civil, and religious life, and men, not women, enjoy privileged access to several spouses at once. The father is not the principal source of authority within the family, but neither is the mother. The authoritarian figure in matrilineal families is another male: the mother's brother (or mother's mother's brother or mother's mother's sister's son).

It is the prevalence of warfare that ruins the logic upon which the prediction of matriarchy is premised. Women are theoretically capable of resisting and even subduing the males they themselves have nurtured and socialized, but males reared in another village or tribe present a different sort of challenge. As soon as males for whatever reason begin to bear the burden of intergroup conflict, women have no choice but to rear large numbers of fierce males of their own.

Male supremacy is a case of "positive feedback," or what has been called "deviation amplification"—the kind of process that leads to the head-splitting squeaks of public-address systems that pick up and then reamplify their own signals. The fiercer the males, the greater the amount of warfare, the more such males are needed. Also, the fiercer the males, the more sexually aggressive they become, the more exploited are the females, and the higher the incidence of polygyny—control over several wives by one man. Polygyny in turn intensifies the shortage of women, raises the level of frustration among the junior males, and increases the motivation for going to war. The amplification builds to an excruciating climax; females are held in contempt and killed in infancy, making it necessary for men to go to war to capture wives in order to rear additional numbers of aggressive men.

To understand the relationship between male chauvinism and warfare it is best to examine the lifestyles of a specific group of primitive military sexists. I have chosen the Yanomamo, a group of about 10,000 American Indian tribesmen who inhabit the Brazil/Venezuela border. The Yanomamo have been labeled the "fierce people" by their principal ethnographer, Napoleon Chagnon of Pennsylvania State University. All observers who have ever been in contact with them agree that they are one of the most aggressive, warlike, and male-oriented societies in the world.

By the time a typical Yanomamo male reaches maturity, he is covered with the wounds and scars of innumerable quarrels, duels, and military raids. Although they hold women in great contempt, Yanomamo men are always brawling over real or imagined acts of adultery and broken promises to provide wives. Yanomamo women are also covered with scars and bruises, mostly the result of violent encounters with seducers, rapists, and husbands. No Yanomamo woman escapes the brutal tutelage of the typical hot-tempered, drug-taking Yanomamo warrior-husband. All Yanomamo men physically abuse their wives. Kind husbands merely bruise and mutilate them; the fierce ones wound and kill.

A favorite means of bullying one's wife is to yank on the sticks of cane that women wear through their pierced ear lobes. An irritated husband may yank so hard that the lobe is torn open. While Chagnon was in the field, a man who suspected his wife of committing adultery went further and chopped off both her ears. In a nearby village, another husband chopped a hunk of flesh out of his wife's arm with a machete. Men expect their wives to serve them and their guests and to respond to all requests promptly and without protest. If a woman does not comply quickly enough, her husband may beat her with a piece of firewood, take a swing at her with his machete, or put a glowing stick of wood against her arm. If he is really angry, a husband may shoot a barbed arrow into his wife's calf or buttock. In one case recorded by Chagnon, the arrow went astray, entered the woman's stomach, and brought her close to death. A man named Paruriwa went into a rage when his wife moved too slowly to suit him, grabbed an ax, and swung it at her. She ducked and ran out screaming. Paruriwa threw the ax but it whizzed past her head. He then went after her with his machete and split her hand open before the village headman could intervene.

There is also a lot of completely unprovoked violence

against women. Chagnon thinks that some of this has to do with the need for men to prove to each other that they are capable of deadly assault. It helps a man's "image" if he publicly beats his wife with a club. Women are also simply used as convenient scapegoats. One man who really wanted to vent his anger on his brother shot his own wife instead; he aimed at a nonvital part, but the arrow went astray and killed her.

Women who run away from their husbands can expect only limited protection from their male kinsmen. Most marriages are contracted between men who agree to exchange sisters. A man's brother-in-law tends to be his closest and most important relative. These men spend long hours in each other's company, blowing hallucinogenic powder into each other's nostrils, and lying in the same hammock together. In one case reported by Chagnon, the brother of a runaway wife became so irritated with his sister for disturbing the comradely relationship he enjoyed with her husband that he struck her with his ax.

An important aspect of Yanomamo male supremacy is the monopoly which males exercise over the use of hallucinogenic drugs. By taking these drugs (the most common, *ebene*, is derived from a jungle vine), men get supernatural visions which the women cannot experience. These visions enable males to become shamans, to visit with demons, and to control malevolent forces. Inhaling *ebene* also helps the men to ignore extremes of pain and to overcome their fears during duels and raids. The apparent immunity to pain exhibited during the chest-pounding and head-clubbing contests that I will describe in a moment probably results from the analgesic side effects of drugs. Men who have been "tripping" present a formidable sight before they pass out or lapse into a stupor. Green snot drips from their noses; they make strange growling noises, walk on all fours, and converse with invisible demons.

As in the case of Judeo-Christian traditions, the Yanomamo justify male chauvinism in their origin myth. At the beginning of the world, they say, there were only fierce men, formed from the blood of the moon. Among these early men was one named Kanaborama whose legs became pregnant. Out of Kanaborama's left leg came women and out of his right leg came feminine men—those Yanomamo who are reluctant to duel and who are cowards in battle.

Like other male-dominated cultures, the Yanomamo think menstrual blood is evil and dangerous. When a girl has her first menses they lock her up inside a specially constructed bamboo cage and force her to go without food. Thereafter, she must isolate herself at every menstrual period and remain squatting alone in the shadow of the house.

Yanomamo women are victimized from childhood on. When a girl's little brother hits her, she gets punished if she hits back. Little boys, however, are never punished for hitting anybody. Yanomamo fathers howl with delight when their angry four-year-old sons strike them in the face.

I have considered the possibility that Chagnon's description of Yanomamo sex roles reflects in part the ethnographer's own masculine bias. Fortunately, the Yanomamo have also been studied by a woman. Professor Judith Shapiro of the University of Chicago also emphasizes the essentially passive role of Yanomamo women. She reports that as far as marriage is concerned, men are definitely the exchangers, and women the exchanged. She translates the Yanomamo term for marriage as "dragging something away" and divorce as "throwing something away." She reports that at eight or nine years of age, girls already begin to serve their husbands; they sleep near them, follow them about, and prepare their meals. A man may even attempt intercourse with his eight-year-old bride. Dr. Shapiro witnessed terrifying scenes in which little girls pleaded with their kinsmen to be taken away from their assigned husbands. In one case, the arms of a reluctant bride were pulled from their sockets as her own relatives tugged one way, and her husband's relatives tugged the other.

Chagnon states that Yanomamo women expect to be manhandled by their husbands and that they measure their status as wives by the frequency of minor beatings their husbands give them. Once he overheard two young women discussing their scalp scars. One of them was saying how much the other's husband must really care for her since he had beaten her over the head so often. Referring to her own experience, Dr. Shapiro says that her unscarred and unbruised condition was a source of concern to the Yanomamo women. She says that they decided "that the men I had associated with did not really care for me enough." While we cannot conclude that Yanomamo women want to be beaten, we can say that they *expect* to be beaten. They find it difficult to imagine a world in which husbands would be less brutal.

The peculiar intensity of the Yanomamo male chauvinist syndrome is best expressed in their duels, which require two men to try to hurt each other to the limit of their endurance. Chest-pounding is the favorite form of inflicting this mutual punishment.

Picture a shouting, milling crowd of men, bodies painted

in red and black designs, white feathers glued to their hair, and exposed penises tied with string upright against their bellies. They brandish bows and arrows, axes, clubs, and machetes, rattling and clacking them as they threaten each other. The men, divided into hosts and guests, have assembled in the central clearing of a Yanomamo village, anxiously watched by their women and children, who stay back under the eaves of the large circular communal dwelling. The hosts accuse the guests of stealing from the gardens. The guests shout that the hosts are stingy and that they are keeping the best food for themselves. The guests have already been given their farewell gifts, so why haven't they gone home? Now, to get rid of them, the hosts challenge them to a chest-pounding duel.

A warrior from the host village pushes into the center of the clearing. He spreads his legs apart, puts his hands behind his back, and thrusts his chest toward the opposite group. A second man pushes forward from among the guests and enters the arena. He looks his adversary over calmly and gets him to change his stance. He crooks the target's left arm so that it rests on the head, assesses the new stance, and makes a final adjustment. With his opponent properly situated, the guest puts himself at correct arm's length, firming and deepening his toehold on the hard-packed earth, feinting forward repeatedly to test the distance and check his balance. Then, leaning back like a baseball pitcher, he puts his entire strength and weight behind his clenched fist as it thuds against the target's chest between nipple and shoulder. The struck man staggers, knees buckling, head shaking, but silent and expressionless. His supporters yell and scream, "Another one!" The scene is repeated. The first man, a huge welt already rising on his pectoral muscle, puts himself back into position. His adversary lines him up, tests for distance, leans back, and delivers a second blow to the same spot. The recipient's knees buckle and he sinks to the ground. The attacker waves his arms victoriously over his head and dances around the victim, making fierce growling noises and moving his feet so fast that they are a blur lost in the dust, while his screaming supporters clack their wooden weapons together and bounce up and down from a squatting position. The fallen man's comrades again urge him to absorb more punishment. For every blow that he receives, he will be able to return one. The more he takes, the more he can give in return and the more likely it is that he will be able to cripple his adversary or make him give up. After taking two more blows, the first man's left chest is swollen and red. Amid the delirious howling of his supporters, he now signals that he has had enough, demanding that the adversary stand still to receive his due.

The particular scene I have been describing is based on Napoleon Chagnon's eyewitness account. Like many other chest-pounding duels, it led to an escalation of violence as soon as one group began to get the better of the other. The hosts ran out of usable chests but were unwilling to initiate any peace overtures. So they challenged the guests to another kind of duel: side-slapping. This involves standing still while your opponent strikes you with his open hand just below the ribs. Blows delivered to this area paralyze a person's diaphragm, and the victim sinks to the ground gasping and unconscious. In this particular case, the sight of favorite comrades lying prone in the dust soon enraged both groups, and men on both sides began to arm their arrows with tips of poisoned bamboo. It was getting dark, and the women and children started to wail. Then they ran behind the men, who formed a protective screen. Breathing hard, hosts and guests faced each other across the clearing. Chagnon was watching at the back of a line of bowmen. With intense relief, he saw the guests grab glowing brands of firewood and slowly back out of the village into the blackness of the jungle.

Sometimes there is an intermediate stage in the escalation of chest-pounding duels. The adversaries hold rocks in their fists and strike blows that make the contestants spit up blood. Another way hosts and their allies entertain each other is by holding machete duels. Pairs of adversaries take turns striking each other with the flat of the blade. Even a slight slip results in a serious injury and further violent confrontations.

The next highest level of violence is the club fight. A man with a special grudge against another challenges his adversary to hit him on the head with an eight-to-ten-foot-long pole shaped like a pool cue. The challenger sticks his own pole in the ground, leans on it, and bows his head. His adversary holds his pole by the thin end, whipping the heavy end down on the proffered pate with bone-crushing force. Having sustained one blow, the recipient is entitled to an immediate opportunity to wallop his opponent in the same manner.

Chagnon reports that the typical Yanomamo pate is covered with long ugly scars. Like the Prussians of former times, the Yanomamo are proud of these dueling souvenirs. They shave the top of their heads to keep them in view and rub the bald area with red pigments so that each scar stands out clearly. If a Yanomamo male lives to forty, his head may be crisscrossed by as many as twenty large scars. Viewed from the top, notes Chagnon, the head of a veteran pole dueler "looks like a road map."

Duels are as common between men of the same village as between men from neighboring villages. Even close relatives frequently resort to armed combat to settle disputes. Chagnon observed at least one encounter between a father and son. The young man had eaten some bananas that his father had hung up to ripen. When the theft was discovered, the father became furious, ripped a pole from the rafters of his house, and smashed it down on his son's head. The son ripped out a pole for himself and attacked his father. In a flash, everybody in the village had chosen sides and was flailing away at somebody else. As the fighting became general, the aim deteriorated, resulting in many bashed fingers and bruised shoulders as well as lacerated skulls. These brawls are likely to break out during any duel as soon as the bystanders catch sight of copious quantities of blood.

The Yanomamo recognize one further level of escalation short of a total commitment to homicide—the spear fight. They make spears which consist of six-foot-long saplings that have been peeled, decorated with red and black designs, and sharpened to a long point. These weapons can inflict severe wounds but are relatively inefficient for producing fatalities.

War is the ultimate expression of the Yanomamo's lifestyle. Unlike the Maring, the Yanomamo seem to have no way to establish any kind of secure truce. They enter into a series of alliances with neighboring villages, but intergroup relations are marred by unending mistrust, malicious rumors, and acts of consummate treachery. I have already suggested what kind of entertainment allies offer each other at their feasts. These occasions are supposed to consolidate friendships, but even the best of allies behave in a fierce and aggressive manner in order to leave no doubt about the value of each group's contribution to the alliance. Because of all the strutting, boasting, and sexual display that goes on during a supposedly friendly feast, the outcome remains unpredictable until the last guest has returned home. All participants are also keenly aware of certain celebrated incidents when host villages deliberately planned to massacre their guests or when the guests, anticipating such a possibility, planned to massacre the hosts. In 1950 many kinsmen of the village that hosted the chest-pounding duel I have just described were victims of a famous treacherous feast. They had gone to a village two days' traveling distance from their own to establish a new alliance. Their hosts let them dance on as if nothing were wrong. Later they went inside the house to rest, and were attacked with axes and clubs. Twelve men were killed. As the survivors rushed out of the village they were attacked again by a force that had remained hidden in the jungle. Several more men were killed and injured.

The Yanomamo are always worried about treachery; they make alliances on the basis of the latest ups and downs of military fortune rather than because of any shared set of interests in people or resources. If a village suffers a severe military setback, it can expect to be attacked repeatedly, even by former allies. The best hope for a village that has lost several males in combat is to go to live with its allies. But no group gives shelter for sentimental reasons. In return

The Savage Male

for temporary food and security, allies expect the defeated group to make gifts of their women.

Ambushes, treacherous feasts, and stealthy raids at dawn —these are the characteristic modes of Yanomamo warfare. Once they get over the boasting and dueling phase, their object is to kill as many enemy men and capture as many enemy women as possible, with no loss whatsoever to themselves. On a raid, the Yanomamo warriors approach the enemy stealthily at night, light no fires, and shiveringly await the dawn in the damp jungle darkness. In an extreme act of bravery, a warrior may slip into the enemy village and kill somebody who is asleep in a hammock. Otherwise, the raiders content themselves with killing males who have come out with the women to fetch water from the river. If the enemy is alert and moves about only in large groups, the raiding party blindly showers the village with arrows and then flees back home without waiting to learn the results. Raiding seems to go on incessantly. During Chagnon's stay, one village was raided over twenty-five times in fifteen months. Chagnon's ability to survive under these conditions is nothing short of remarkable—a great tribute to his skill and courage as an ethnographer.

Why do the Yanomamo fight so much? Professor Chagnon himself has not offered satisfactory reasons. Essentially he accepts the explanation that the Yanomamo offer. They say that most duels, raids, and other outbreaks of violence are caused by disputes over women. Women are definitely in short supply. Despite the fact that a quarter of the males die in combat, males outnumber females by 120 to 100. To make matters worse, headmen and others who have a special reputation for fierceness keep as many as four or five wives at one time. Altogether, about 25 percent of the men have two or more wives. Since fathers betroth their infant daughters to senior influential figures to gain favors or to reciprocate their own marriages, all the sexually mature women in the village are married. This leaves many young men without any source of heterosexual gratification other than adultery. Young fierce-males-to-be make trysts with disgruntled or intimidated wives in the evening. The next morning they meet under cover of the jungle when many people leave the village to defecate and urinate.

A Yanomamo husband will gladly share one of his wives with junior brothers and comrades. But males who obtain access to women through wife-lending place themselves in debt to the husband and will have to repay him with services or women captured in battle. A young man seeking a reputation must not put himself in a position of dependency; he prefers instead to cajole and intimidate the village's married women into clandestine arrangements. Since Yanomamo girls are betrothed even before they begin to menstruate, all young Yanomamo males actively covet their neighbor's wives. Yanomamo husbands become enraged when they discover a tryst, not so much because of sexual jealousy but because the adulterous male should have compensated the husband with gifts and services.

The capture of women during raids on enemy villages is one of the prime objectives of Yanomamo warfare. As soon as a successful raiding party feels safe from pursuit, the warriors gang-rape the female captives. When they reach the raider's village, they hand the women over to the men who stayed home and these gang-rape them again. Later after much haggling and arguing, the raiders assign the captives to be wives to particular warriors.

One of the most terrifying stories to come out of Yanomamoland is that told by Helena Valero, a Brazilian woman who was caught by a Yanomamo raiding party when she was ten years old. Soon afterward, the men who had captured her began to fight among themselves. One faction routed the other, killed all the small children by bashing their heads against the rocks, and marched the surviving females home. Helena Valero spent most of the rest of her childhood and youth running away from one group of raiders only to be caught by another, then running away again, hiding in the jungle from her pursuers, and being recaptured and assigned to different husbands. She was wounded twice by curare-tipped arrows, and bore several children before she finally managed to escape to a missionary settlement on the Orinoco River.

The shortage of women, infant betrothal, adultery, polygyny, and the taking of female captives all seem to point to sex as the cause of Yanomamo war. Yet I find one nagging, stubborn fact that this theory cannot explain: the shortage of women is artificially created. The Yanomamo steadily kill off a large percentage of their female babies, not only through selective neglect but through specific acts of murder.

Men demand that their first-born child be a male. Women kill their daughters until they can present a male child. Thereafter, infants of both sexes may be killed. Yanomamo women kill their babies by strangling them with vines, by standing on both ends of a stick placed on top of the baby's throat, by banging the baby's head against a tree, or by simply leaving the infant to fend for itself on the jungle floor. The net effect of infanticide and more benign forms of sexual selection is a juvenile sex ratio of 154 males to 100 females. Given the hardships that men must endure to get a wife for themselves, there must be a very strong force—a force other than sex and more powerful—that leads them to destroy the very source and object of all their lusts and struggles.

The mystifying feature of infanticide and warfare in Yanomamoland is the apparent absence of population pressure and a seeming superabundance of resources. The Yanomamo derive their main source of food calories from the plantains and the banana trees that grow in their forest gardens. Like the Maring, they must burn the forest to get these gardens started. But bananas and plantains are not like yams or sweet potatoes. They are perennials that provide high yields per unit of labor input for many consecutive years. Since the Yanomamo live in the midst of the world's greatest tropical forest, the little burning that they do scarcely threatens to "eat up the trees." A typical Yanomamo village has only 100 to 200 people in it, a population which could easily grow enough bananas or plantains in nearby garden sites without ever having to move. Yet the Yanomamo villages are constantly on the move, splitting up and moving their gardens at a much higher rate than other slash-and-burn Amazon forest peoples.

Chagnon says that they split up and move so often because they fight over women and are always at war. I suggest that it is more nearly correct to say that they fight over women and are always at war because they move so often. The Yanomamo are not typical cut-and-burn horticulturalists. Their ancestors were nomadic hunters and gatherers living away from the main rivers in small scattered bands that relied on wild forest products for their chief source of subsistence. We can be certain that only in more or less recent times did they begin to depend on bananas and plantains as their staple ᴀoods, since these plants were brought to the New World by Portuguese and Spanish settlers. Until recent times, the maᴀn centers of the American Indian populations in the Amazon were located along the major rivers and their tributaries. Tribes like the Yanomamo lived in the backlands and kept out of sight of the riverine peoples, who had big permanent villages and canoes that made them highly mobile. Toward the end of the nineteenth century the last of the large riverine Indian villages were destroyed as a result of the rubber trade and the spread of Brazilian and Venezuelan settlements. The only Indians who survived over extensive areas of the Amazon were "foot" Indians, whose nomadic way of life protected them from the white man's guns and diseases.

To this day the Yanomamo exhibit unmistakable signs of their recent "foot" Indian way of life. They do not know how to construct or paddle canoes, although their main settlements are now on the banks of or close by the Orinoco and Mavaca rivers. They do little fishing, although such waters are usually rich in fish and aquatic animals. They lack knowledge of how to make cooking pots, although plantains are best prepared by boiling. And finally, they don't know how to manufacture stone axes, although they are now dependent upon steel axes for making their plantain gardens.

Let me give a somewhat speculative account of recent Yanomamo history. The nomadic Yanomamo who lived in the remote mountains between Venezuela and Brazil began to experiment with banana and plantain gardens. These crops yielded a great increase in the amount of food calories per capita. As a result, the population of the Yanomamo also began to increase—today they are one of the most populous Indian groups in the entire Amazon basin. But plantain and bananas have one striking defect: they are notoriously deficient in proteins. Formerly, as nomadic hunters, the Yanomamo had easily satisfied their need for protein by eating forest animals, including tapir, deer, peccary, anteaters, armadillos, monkeys, pacas, agoutis, crocodiles, lizards, snakes, and turtles. With the increase in human population density caused by the efficient garden crops, these animals were hunted with unprecedented intensity. As is well known, forest animal populations are easily exterminated or driven away by intensive hunting. In pre-contact times, Amazonian tribes with dense populations avoided a similar consequence by exploiting the fish of their riverine habitats. The Yanomamo, however, were not able to do this.

Amazonian specialists Jane and Eric Ross suggest that protein scarcities and not libidinal surpluses account for the constant fissioning and feuding among Yanomamo villages. I agree. The Yanomamo have "eaten the forest"—not its trees, but its animals—and they are suffering the consequences in terms of increased warfare, treachery, and infanticide, and a brutal sex life.

The Yanomamo themselves have two words for hunger—one denotes an empty stomach, while the other denotes a full stomach that craves meat. Meat hunger is a constant theme of Yanomamo song and poetry, and meat is the focus of Yanomamo feasting. In Helena Valero's account of her captivity, one of the few ways that a Yanomamo woman

The Savage Male

could make a man cringe was to complain about his poor performance as a hunter. Hunters must range farther and farther from Yanomamo villages in order not to return empty-handed. Expeditions of ten or twelve days are required in order to bring back substantial numbers of large animals. Chagnon himself tells of going along on a hunting expedition lasting five days in an area that had "not been hunted in decades" without collecting enough meat to feed even the members of the expedition. Since the typical Yanomamo village is less than a day's walk from its nearest neighbor, extended expeditions inevitably cross and recross hunting territories that are used by villages other than one's own. These villages compete for the same scarce resource, and that resource is not women but protein.

I prefer this solution to the riddle of the savage male because it explains in practical terms why Yanomamo women actively collaborate in their own exploitation by killing and neglecting more female than male babies. It is true that Yanomamo men prefer sons to daughters. A woman who disappoints her husband by not rearing sons would undoubtedly fall into disfavor with him and risk being beaten more often. Yet I think that Yanomamo women could easily reverse the sex ratio to favor females against males if it was in their interest to do so. Women give birth in the forest, away from the village, with no men present. This means that they could practice selective infanticide against males with impunity after the birth of their first son. In addition, they have endless opportunities to practice selective neglect against all their male children without risk of discovery or retaliation by their husbands.

I can cite at least one good example of how women could

exercise sovereign control over sex ratios in the Yanomamö nursery. Chagnon says that he once saw a "plump, well-fed young mother" eating food (probably plantain mash) that could easily be eaten by an infant. Next to her was her "emaciated, filthy, and nearly starved" two-year-old son, who kept reaching out for some of this food. Chagnon asked the mother why she wasn't feeding her baby, and she explained that it had gotten a bad case of diarrhea some time previously and had stopped nursing. As a result, the woman's milk had dried up and there was nothing to give it. No other foods would help, she said, because "it did not know how to eat other foods." Chagnon then "insisted that she share her food with the child." The baby ate the food ravenously, leading Chagnon to the conclusion that "she was letting the baby die slowly of starvation."

The practical and mundane reason for the systematic killing and neglect of more female than male children can't be simply that the men force the women to do it. There are too many opportunities, as the example I have just given illustrates, to evade and circumvent the men's wishes in this matter. Rather, the effective basis of Yanomamö women's nursery practices is their own interest in raising more boys than girls. This interest is rooted in the fact that there are already too many Yanomamö in relation to their ability to exploit their habitat. A higher ratio of men to women means more protein per capita (because men are the hunters) and a slower rate of population growth. It also means more warfare, but for the Yanomamö, as for the Maring, warfare is the price paid for raising sons when they can't raise daughters. Only, the Yanomamö pay more heavily for this privilege, since they have already degraded the carrying capacity of their habitat.

Some women's liberationists who acknowledge the role of warfare in relation to sexism insist nonetheless that women are the victims of a male conspiracy because only men are taught how to kill with weapons. Why, they wish to know, should women not also be taught warrior skills? Would not a Yanomamo village in which both men and women wielded bows and clubs be a more formidable fighting force than one in which women merely huddle in the shadows awaiting their fate?

Why should the effort at brutalization be concentrated on the males? Why not teach both males and females how to handle the technology of aggression? These are important questions. I think the answer has to do with the problem of training human beings—either male or female—to be mean and ferocious. As I see it, there are two classical strategies by which societies make people brutal. One is to encourage brutality by giving food, comfort, and bodily health as rewards to the most brutal personalities. The other is to allot the greatest sexual rewards and privileges to the most brutal personalities. Of these two strategies, the second is the more effective because the deprivation of food, comfort, and bodily health is militarily counterproductive. The Yanomamo need highly motivated killers, but they must be strong and robust if they are to have redeeming social functions. Sex is the best reinforcement for conditioning brutal personalities because sexual deprivation enhances rather than diminishes the ability to fight.

My argument here runs counter to much pseudoscience

conceived in the image of our own tribal male chauvinists such as Sigmund Freud, Konrad Lorenz, and Robert Ardrey. Our received wisdom in this matter is that males are naturally more aggressive and ferocious because the male sex role is naturally an aggressive one. But the link between sex and aggression is as artificial as the link between infanticide and war. Sex is a source of aggressive energy and brutal behavior only because male chauvinist social systems expropriate sexual rewards, allocate them to aggressive males, and deny them to passive, nonaggressive ones.

Frankly, I see no reason why the same sort of brutalization could not be imposed on women. The myth of the instinctively passive, tender, motherly female is simply an echo set up by male chauvinist mythology concerning instinctively brutal males. If only fierce "masculinized" females were permitted to have sexual relations with males, we would have no trouble in getting everybody to believe that females are naturally aggressive and brutal.

If sex is to be used to energize and control aggressive behavior, then it follows that both sexes cannot simultaneously be brutalized to an equal degree. One or the other must be trained to be dominant. It cannot be both. To brutalize both is to invite a literal war of the sexes. Among the Yanomamo this would mean armed struggle between men and women for control over each other as a reward for their battlefield exploits. In other words, to make sex a reward for bravery, one of the sexes has to be taught cowardice.

These considerations lead me to a slight emendation of the liberationist's paradigm "Anatomy is not destiny." Human anatomy *is* destiny under certain conditions. When warfare was a prominent means of population control, and when the technology of warfare consisted primarily of primitive hand-held weapons, male chauvinist lifestyles were necessarily ascendant. Insofar as neither of these conditions is true of today's world, liberationists are correct in predicting the decline of male chauvinist lifestyles. I would add that the rate of this decline and the ultimate prospects for sexual equality depend upon the further elimination of conventional police and military forces. Let us hope that this occurs as a result of the elimination of the need for police or military personnel rather than as a result of perfecting battle tactics that don't depend on physical strength. We should have gone little beyond the Yanomamo if the net outcome of the sexual revolution is a secure position for women at the head of the mace squads or in the nuclear command posts.

Potlatch

SOME OF the most puzzling lifestyles on exhibit in the museum of world ethnography bear the imprint of a strange craving known as the "drive for prestige." Some people seem to hunger for approval as others hunger for meat. The puzzling thing is not that people hunger for approval, but that occasionally their craving seems to become so powerful that they begin to compete with each other for prestige as others compete for land or protein or sex. Sometimes this competition grows so fierce that it appears to become an end in itself. It then takes on the appearance of an obsession wholly divorced from, and even directly opposed to, rational calculations of material costs.

Vance Packard struck a responsive chord when he described the United States as a nation of competitive status seekers. Many Americans seem to spend their entire lives trying to climb further up the social pyramid simply in order to impress each other. We seem to be more interested in working in order to get people to admire us for our wealth

111

than in the actual wealth itself, which often enough consists of chromium baubles and burdensome or useless objects. It is amazing how much effort people are willing to spend to obtain what Thorstein Veblen described as the vicarious thrill of being mistaken for members of a class that doesn't have to work. Veblen's mordant phrases "conspicuous consumption" and "conspicuous waste" aptly convey a sense of the peculiarly intense desire for "keeping up with the Joneses" that lies behind the ceaseless cosmetic alterations in the automotive, appliance, and clothing industries.

Early in the present century, anthropologists were surprised to discover that certain primitive tribes engaged in conspicuous consumption and conspicuous waste to a degree unmatched by even the most wasteful of modern consumer economies. Ambitious, status-hungry men were found competing with each other for approval by giving huge feasts. The rival feast givers judged each other by the amount of food they provided, and a feast was a success only if the guests could eat until they were stupefied, stagger off into the bush, stick their fingers down their throats, vomit, and come back for more.

The most bizarre instance of status seeking was discovered among the American Indians who formerly inhabited the coastal regions of Southern Alaska, British Columbia, and Washington. Here the status seekers practiced what seems like a maniacal form of conspicuous consumption and conspicuous waste known as *potlatch*. The object of potlatch was to give away or destroy more wealth than one's rival. If the potlatch giver was a powerful chief, he might attempt to shame his rivals and gain everlasting admiration from his followers by destroying food, clothing, and money. Some-

112

times he might even seek prestige by burning down his own house.

Potlatch was made famous by Ruth Benedict in her book *Patterns of Culture*, which describes how potlatch operated among the Kwakiutl, the aboriginal inhabitants of Vancouver Island. Benedict thought that potlatch was part of a megalomaniacal lifestyle characteristic of Kwakiutl culture in general. It was the "cup" God had given them to drink from. Ever since, potlatch has been a monument to the belief that cultures are the creations of inscrutable forces and deranged personalities. As a result of reading *Patterns of Culture*, experts in many fields concluded that the drive for prestige makes a shambles of attempts to explain lifestyles in terms of practical and mundane factors.

I want to show here that the Kwakiutl potlatch was not the result of maniacal whims, but of definite economic and ecological conditions. When these conditions are absent, the need to be admired and the drive for prestige express themselves in completely different lifestyle practices. Inconspicuous consumption replaces conspicuous consumption, conspicuous waste is forbidden, and there are no competitive status seekers.

The Kwakiutl used to live in plank-house villages set close to the shore in the midst of cedar and fir rain forests. They fished and hunted along the island-studded sounds and fiords of Vancouver in huge dugout canoes. Always eager to attract traders, they made their villages conspicuous by erecting on the beach the carved tree trunks we erroneously call "totem poles." The carvings on these poles symbolized the ancestral titles to which the chiefs of the village laid claim.

113

A Kwakiutl chief was never content with the amount of respect he was getting from his own followers and from neighboring chiefs. He was always insecure about his status. True enough, the family titles to which he laid claim belonged to his ancestors. But there were other people who could trace descent from the same ancestors and who were entitled to vie with him for recognition as a chief. Every chief therefore felt the obligation to justify and validate his chiefly pretensions. The prescribed manner for doing this was to hold potlatches. Each potlatch was given by a host chief and his followers to a guest chief and his followers. The object of the potlatch was to show that the host chief was truly entitled to chiefly status and that he was more exalted than the guest chief. To prove this point, the host chief gave the rival chief and his followers quantities of valuable gifts. The guests would belittle what they received and vow to hold a return potlatch at which their own chief would prove that he was greater than the former host by giving back even larger quantities of more valuable gifts.

Preparations for potlatch required the accumulation of fresh and dried fish, fish oil, berries, animal skins, blankets, and other valuables. On the appointed day, the guests paddled up to the host village and went into the chief's house. There they gorged themselves on salmon and wild berries while dancers masked as beaver gods and thunderbirds entertained them.

The host chief and his followers arranged in neat piles the wealth that was to be given away. The visitors stared at their host sullenly as he pranced up and down, boasting about how much he was about to give them. As he counted out the boxes of fish oil, baskets full of berries, and piles of blankets, he commented derisively on the poverty of his rivals. Laden with gifts, the guests finally were free to paddle back to their own village. Stung to the quick, the guest chief and his followers vowed to get even. This could only be achieved by inviting their rivals to a return potlatch and obliging them to accept even greater amounts of valuables than they had given away. Considering all the Kwakiutl villages as a single unit, potlatch stimulated a ceaseless flow of prestige and valuables moving in opposite directions.

An ambitious chief and his followers had potlatch rivals in several different villages at once. Specialists in counting property kept track of what had to be done in each village in order to even the score. If a chief managed to get the better of his rivals in one place, he still had to confront his adversaries in another.

At the potlatch, the host chief would say things like, "I am the only great tree. Bring your counter of property that he may try in vain to count the property that is to be given away." Then the chief's followers demanded silence from the guests with the warning: "Do not make any noise, tribes. Be quiet or we shall cause a landslide of wealth from our chief, the overhanging mountain." At some potlatches blankets and other valuables were not given away but were destroyed. Sometimes successful potlatch chiefs decided to hold "grease feasts" at which boxes of oil obtained from the candlefish were poured on the fire in the center of the house. As the flames roared up, dark grease smoke filled the room. The guests sat impassively or even complained about the chill in the air while the wealth destroyer ranted, "I am the only one on earth—the only one in the whole world who makes this smoke rise from the beginning of the year to the end for the invited tribes." At some grease feasts the flames ignited the planks in the roof and an entire house would become a potlatch offering, causing the greatest shame to the guests and much rejoicing among the hosts.

According to Ruth Benedict, potlatching was caused by the obsessive status hunger of the Kwakiutl chiefs. "Judged by the standards of other cultures the speeches of their chiefs are unabashed megalomania," she wrote. "The object of all Kwakiutl enterprises was to show oneself superior to one's rivals." In her opinion, the whole aboriginal economic system of the Pacific Northwest was "bent to the service of this obsession."

I think that Benedict was mistaken. The economic system of the Kwakiutl was not bent to the service of status rivalry; rather, status rivalry was bent to the service of the economic system.

All of the basic ingredients of the Kwakiutl giveaways, except for their destructive aspects, are present in primitive societies widely dispersed over different parts of the globe. Stripped down to its elementary core, the potlatch is a competitive feast, a nearly universal mechanism for assuring the production and distribution of wealth among peoples who have not yet fully acquired a ruling class.

Melanesia and New Guinea present the best opportunity to study competitive feasting under relatively pristine conditions. Throughout this region, there are so-called big men who owe their superior status to the large number of feasts that each has sponsored during his lifetime. Each feast has to be preceded by an intensive effort on the part of an aspiring big man to accumulate the necessary wealth.

Among the Kaoka-speaking people of the Solomon Islands,

for example, the status-hungry individual begins his career by making his wife and children plant larger yam gardens. As described by the Australian anthropologist Ian Hogbin, the Kaoka who wants to become a big man then gets his kinsmen and his age-mates to help him fish. Later he begs sows from his friends and increases the size of his pig herd. As the litters are born he boards additional animals among his neighbors. Soon his relatives and friends feel that the young man is going to be a success. They see his large gardens and his big pig herd and they redouble their own efforts to make the forthcoming feast a memorable one. When he becomes a big man they want the young candidate to remember that they helped him. Finally, they all get together and build an extra-fine house. The men go off on one last fishing expedition. The women harvest yams and collect firewood, banana leaves, and coconuts. As the guests arrive (as in the case of potlatch), the wealth is stacked in neat piles and put on display for everyone to count and admire.

On the day of the feast given by a young man named Atana, Hogbin counted the following items: 250 pounds of dried fish, 3,000 yam and coconut cakes, 11 large bowls of yam pudding, and 8 pigs. All this was the direct result of the extra work effort organized by Atana. But some of the guests themselves, anticipating an important occasion, brought presents to be added to the giveaway. Their contributions raised the total to 300 pounds of fish, 5,000 cakes, 19 bowls of pudding and 13 pigs. Atana proceeded to divide this wealth into 257 portions, one each for every person who had helped him or who had brought gifts, rewarding some more than others. "Only the remnants were left for Atana himself," notes Hogbin. This is normal for status seekers in Guadalcanal, who always say: "The giver of the feast takes the bones and the stale cakes; the meat and the fat go to the others."

The feast-giving days of the big man, like those of the potlatch chiefs, are never over. On threat of being reduced to commoner status, each big man is obliged to busy himself with plans and preparations for the next feast. Since there are several big men per village and community, these plans and preparations often lead to complex competitive maneuvering for the allegiance of relatives and neighbors. The big men work harder, worry more, and consume less than anybody else. Prestige is their only reward.

The big man can be described as a worker-entrepreneur— the Russians call them "Stakhanovites"—who renders important services to society by raising the level of production. As a result of the big man's craving for status, more people work harder and produce more food and other valuables.

Under conditions where everyone has equal access to the means of subsistence, competitive feasting serves the practical function of preventing the labor force from falling back to levels of productivity that offer no margin of safety in crises such as war and crop failures. Furthermore, since there are no formal political institutions capable of integrating independent villages into a common economic framework, competitive feasting creates an extensive network of economic expectations. This has the effect of pooling the productive effort of larger populations than can be mobilized by any given village. Finally, competitive feasting by big men acts as an automatic equalizer of annual fluctuations in productivity among a series of villages that occupy different microenvironments—seacoast, lagoon, or upland habitats. Automatically, the biggest feasts in any given year will be hosted by villages that have enjoyed conditions of rainfall, temperature, and humidity most favorable to production.

All of these points apply to the Kwakiutl. The Kwakiutl chiefs were like Melanesian big men except that they operated with a much more productive technological inventory in a richer environment. Like big men, they competed with each other to attract men and women to their villages. The greatest chiefs were the best providers and gave the biggest potlatches. The chief's followers shared vicariously in his prestige and helped him to achieve more exalted honors. The chiefs commissioned the carving of the "totem poles." These were in fact grandiose advertisements proclaiming by their height and bold designs that here was a village with a mighty chief who could cause great works to be done, and who could protect his followers from famine and disease. In claiming hereditary rights to the animal crests carved on the poles, the chiefs were actually saying that they were great providers of food and comfort. Potlatch was a means of telling their rivals to put up or shut up.

Despite the overt competitive thrust of potlatch, it functioned aboriginally to transfer food and other valuables from centers of high productivity to less fortunate villages. I should put this even more strongly: Because of the competitive thrust, such transfers were assured. Since there were unpredictable fluctuations in fish runs, wild fruit and vegetable harvests, intervillage potlatching was advantageous from the standpoint of the regional population as a whole. When the fish spawned in nearby streams and the berries ripened close at hand, last year's guests became this year's hosts. Aboriginally, potlatch meant that each year the haves gave and the have-nots took. To eat, all a have-not had to do was admit that the rival chief was a great man.

Why did the practical basis of potlatch escape the attention of Ruth Benedict? Anthropologists began to study potlatch only long after the aboriginal peoples of the Pacific Northwest had entered into commercial and wage-labor relations with Russian, English, Canadian, and American merchants and settlers. This contact rapidly gave rise to epidemics of smallpox and other European diseases that killed off a large part of the native population. For example, the population of the Kwakiutl fell from 23,000 in 1836 to 2,000 in 1886. The decline automatically intensified the competition for manpower. At the same time, wages paid by the Europeans pumped unprecedented amounts of wealth into the potlatch network. From the Hudson's Bay Company, the Kwakiutl received thousands of trade blankets in exchange for animal skins. At the great potlatches these blankets replaced food as the most important item to be given away. The dwindling population soon found itself with more blankets and other valuables than it could consume. Yet the need to attract followers was greater than ever due to the labor shortage. So the potlatch chiefs ordered the destruction of property in the vain hope that such spectacular demonstrations of wealth would bring the people back to the empty villages. But these were the practices of a dying culture struggling to adapt to a new set of political and economic conditions; they bore little resemblance to the potlatch of aboriginal times.

Competitive feasting thought about, narrated, and imagined by the participants is very different from competitive feasting viewed as an adaptation to material constraints and opportunities. In the social dreamwork—the lifestyle consciousness of the participants—competitive feasting is a manifestation of the big man's or potlatch chief's insatiable craving for prestige. But from the point of view followed in this book, the insatiable craving for prestige is a manifestation of competitive feasting. Every society makes use of the need for approval, but not every society links prestige to success in competitive feasting.

Competitive feasting as a source of prestige must be seen in evolutionary perspective to be properly understood. Big men like Atana or the Kwakiutl chiefs carry out a form of economic exchange known as redistribution. That is, they gather together the results of the productive effort of many individuals and then redistribute the aggregated wealth in different quantities to a different set of people. As I have said, the Kaoka redistributor-big man works harder, worries more, and consumes less than anybody else in the village. This is not true of the Kwakiutl chief-redistributor. The great potlatch chiefs performed the entrepreneurial and managerial functions that were necessary for a big potlatch, but aside from an occasional fishing or sea-lion expedition, they left the hardest work to their followers. The greatest potlatch chiefs even had a few war captives working for them as slaves. From the point of view of consumption privileges, the Kwakiutl chiefs had begun to reverse the Kaoka formula and were keeping some of the "meat and fat" for themselves, leaving most of the "bones and stale cakes" for their followers.

Continuing along the evolutionary line leading from Atana, the impoverished worker-entrepreneur big man, to the semihereditary Kwakiutl chiefs, we end up with state-level

societies ruled over by hereditary kings who perform no
basic industrial or agricultural labor and who keep the most
and best of everything for themselves. At the imperial level,
exalted divine-right rulers maintain their prestige by building conspicuous palaces, temples, and mega-monuments, and
validate their right to hereditary privileges against all
challengers—not by potlatch, but by force of arms. Reversing direction, we can go from kings to potlatch chiefs to
big men, back to egalitarian lifestyles in which all competitive displays and conspicuous consumption by individuals
disappear, and anyone foolish enough to boast about how
great he is gets accused of witchcraft and is stoned to death.

In the truly egalitarian societies that have survived long
enough to be studied by anthropologists, redistribution in
the form of competitive feasting does not occur. Instead, the
mode of exchange known as reciprocity predominates.
Reciprocity is the technical term for an economic exchange
that takes place between two individuals in which neither
specifies precisely what is expected in return nor when they
expect it. Superficially, reciprocal exchanges don't look like
exchanges at all. The expectation of one party and obligation
of the other remain unstated. One party can continue to take
from the other for quite a while with no resistance from the
giver and no embarrassment in the taker. Nonetheless, the
transaction cannot be considered a pure gift. There is an
underlying expectation of return, and if the balance between
two individuals gets too far out of line, eventually the giver
will start to grumble and gossip. Concern will be shown for
the taker's health and sanity, and if the situation does not
improve, people begin to suspect that the taker is possessed
by malevolent spirits or is practicing witchcraft. In egali-

tarian societies, individuals who consistently violate the rules of reciprocity are in fact likely to be psychotic and a menace to their community.

We can get some idea of what reciprocal exchanges are like by thinking about the way we exchange goods and services with our close friends or relatives. Brothers, for example, are not supposed to calculate the precise dollar value of everything they do for each other. They should feel free to borrow each other's shirts or phonograph albums and ought not to hesitate to ask for favors. In brotherhood and friendship both parties accept the principle that if one has to give more than he takes, it will not affect the solidary relationship between them. If one friend invites another to dinner, there should be no hesitation in giving or accepting a second or a third invitation even if the first dinner still remains unreciprocated. Yet there is a limit to that sort of thing, because after a while unreciprocated gift-giving begins to feel suspiciously like exploitation. In other words, everybody likes to be thought generous, but nobody wants to be taken for a sucker. This is precisely the quandary we get ourselves into at Christmas when we attempt to revert to the principle of reciprocity in drawing up our shopping lists. The gift can neither be too cheap nor too expensive; and yet our calculations must appear entirely casual, so we remove the price tag.

But to really see reciprocity in action you must live in an egalitarian society that doesn't have money and where nothing can be bought or sold. Everything about reciprocity is opposed to precise counting and reckoning of what one person owes to another. In fact, the whole idea is to deny that anybody really owes anything. One can tell if a lifestyle is based on reciprocity or something else by whether or not people say thank you. In truly egalitarian societies, it is rude to be openly grateful for the receipt of material goods or services. Among the Semai of central Malaya, for example, no one ever expresses gratitude for the meat that a hunter gives away in exactly equal portions to his companions. Robert Dentan, who has lived with the Semai, found that to say thank you was very rude because it suggested either that you were calculating the size of the piece of meat you had been given, or that you were surprised by the success and generosity of the hunter.

In contrast to the conspicuous display put on by the Kaoka big man, and the boastful ranting of potlatch chiefs, and our own flaunting of status symbols, the Semai follow a lifestyle in which those who are most successful must be the least conspicuous. In their egalitarian lifestyle, status seeking through rivalrous redistribution or any form of conspicuous consumption or conspicuous waste is literally unthinkable. Egalitarian peoples are repelled and frightened by the faintest suggestion that they are being treated generously or that one person thinks he's better than another.

Professor Richard Lee of the University of Toronto tells an amusing story about the meaning of reciprocal exchange among egalitarian hunters and gatherers. For the better part of a year, Lee had been following the Bushmen around the Kalahari Desert observing what they ate. The Bushmen were very cooperative and Lee wanted to show his gratitude, but he had nothing to give them that would not disturb their normal diet and pattern of activity. As Christmas approached he learned that the Bushmen were likely to camp at the edge of the desert near villages from which they sometimes obtained meat through trade. With the intention of giving them an ox for a Christmas present, he drove about in his jeep from one village to another, trying to find the biggest ox that he could buy. In a remote village, Lee finally located an animal of monstrous proportions, one covered with a thick layer of fat. Like many primitive peoples, the Bushmen crave fatty meat because the animals they obtain by hunting are usually lean and stringy. Returning to camp, Lee took his Bushmen friends aside and told them one by one that he had bought the largest ox he had ever seen and that he was going to let them slaughter it at Christmas time.

The first man to hear the good news became visibly alarmed. He asked Lee where he had bought the ox, what color it was, and what size its horns were, and then he shook his head. "I know that ox," he said. "Why, it is nothing but skin and bones! You must have been drunk to buy such a worthless animal!" Convinced that his friend didn't really know what ox he was talking about, Lee confided in several other Bushmen, but continued to meet with the same astonished reaction: "You bought that worthless animal? Of course we will eat it," each would say, "but it won't fill us up. We will eat and go home to bed with stomachs rumbling." When Christmas came and the ox was finally slaughtered, the beast turned out to be covered with a thick layer of fat, and it was devoured with great gusto. There was more than enough meat and fat for everybody. Lee went over to his friends and insisted upon an explanation. "Yes, of course we knew all along what the ox was really like," one hunter admitted. "But when a young man kills much meat he comes to think of himself as a chief or big man, and he thinks of the rest of us as his servants or inferiors. We cannot accept this," he went on. "We refuse one who boasts, for someday his pride will make him kill somebody. So we always speak of his meat as worthless. This way we cool his heart and make him gentle."

The Eskimos explained their fear of boastful and generous gift-givers with the proverb "Gifts make slaves just as whips make dogs." And that is exactly what happened. In evolutionary perspective, the gift-givers at first gave gifts that came from their own extra work; soon people found themselves working harder to reciprocate and to make it possible for the gift-givers to give them more gifts; eventually the gift-givers became very powerful, and they no longer needed to obey the rules of reciprocity. They could force people to pay taxes and to work for them without actually redistributing what was in their storehouses and palaces. Of course, as assorted modern big men and politicians occasionally recognize, it is still easier to get "slaves" to work for you if you give them an occasional big feast instead of whipping them all the time.

If people like the Eskimo, Bushmen, and Semai understood the dangers of gift-giving, why did others permit the gift-givers to flourish? And why were big men permitted to get so puffed up that they could turn around and enslave the very people whose work made their glory possible? Once again, I suspect that I am on the verge of trying to explain everything at once. But permit me to make a few suggestions.

Reciprocity is a form of economic exchange that is primarily adapted to conditions in which the stimulation of intensive extra productive effort would have an adverse effect upon group survival. These conditions are found among certain hunters and gatherers such as the Eskimo, Semai, and Bushmen, whose survival depends entirely on the vigor of the natural communities of plants and animals in their habitat. If hunters suddenly engage in a concerted effort to capture more animals and uproot more plants, they risk permanently impairing the supply of game in their territory.

Lee found, for example, that his Bushmen worked at subsistence for only ten to fifteen hours a week. This discovery effectively destroys one of the shoddiest myths of industrial society—namely that we have more leisure today than ever before. Primitive hunters and gatherers work less than we do—without benefit of a single labor union— because their ecosystems cannot tolerate weeks and months of intensive extra effort. Among the Bushmen, Stakhanovite personalities who would run about getting friends and relatives to work harder by promising them a big feast would constitute a definite menace to society. If he got his followers to work like the Kaoka for a month, an aspiring Bushman big man would kill or scare off every game animal for miles around and starve his people to death before the end of the year. So reciprocity and not redistribution predominates among the Bushmen, and the highest prestige falls to the quietly dependable hunter who never boasts about his achievements and who avoids any hint that he is giving a gift when he divides up an animal he has killed.

Competitive feasting and other forms of redistribution overwhelmed the primordial reliance upon reciprocity when it became possible to increase the duration and intensity of work without inflicting irreversible damage upon the habitat's carrying capacity. Typically this became possible when domesticated plants and animals were substituted for natural food resources. Within broad limits, the more work you put into planting and raising domesticated species, the more food you can produce. The only hitch is that people don't usually work harder than they have to. Redistribution was the answer to this problem. Redistribution began to appear as people worked harder in order to maintain a reciprocal balance with prestige-hungry, overzealous producers. As the reciprocal exchanges became unbalanced, they became gifts; and as the gifts piled up, the gift-givers were rewarded with prestige and counter-gifts. Soon redistribution predominated over reciprocity and highest prestige went to the most boastful, calculating gift-givers, who cajoled, shamed, and ultimately forced everybody to work harder than the Bushman ever dreamed was possible.

As the example of the Kwakiutl indicates, conditions appropriate for the development of competitive feasting and redistribution sometimes also occurred among nonagricultural populations. Among the coastal peoples of the Pacific Northwest, annual runs of salmon, other migratory fish, and sea mammals provided the ecological analogue of agricultural harvests. The salmon or candlefish ran in such vast numbers that if people worked harder they could always catch more fish. Moreover, as long as they fished with the aboriginal dip net, they could never catch enough fish to influence the spawning runs and deplete next year's supply.

Stepping away for the moment from our examination of reciprocal and redistributive prestige systems, we can surmise that every major type of political and economic system uses prestige in a distinctive manner. For example, with the appearance of capitalism in Western Europe, competitive acquisition of wealth once more became the fundamental criterion for big-man status. Only in this case, the big men tried to take away each other's wealth, and highest prestige and power went to the individual who managed to accumulate and hold onto the greatest fortune. During the early years of capitalism, highest prestige went to those who were richest but lived most frugally. After their fortunes had become more secure, the capitalist upper class resorted to grand-scale conspicuous consumption and conspicuous waste in order to impress their rivals. They built great mansions, dressed in exclusive finery, adorned themselves with huge jewels, and spoke contemptuously of the impoverished masses. Meanwhile, the middle and lower classes continued to award highest prestige to those who worked hardest, spent least, and soberly resisted all forms of conspicuous consumption and conspicuous waste. But as the growth of industrial capacity began to saturate the consumer market, the middle and lower classes had to be weaned away from their frugal habits. Advertising and mass media joined forces to induce the middle and lower classes to stop saving and to buy, consume, waste, destroy, or otherwise get rid of ever-larger quantities of goods and services. And so among middle-class status seekers, highest prestige now goes to the biggest and most conspicuous consumer.

But in the meantime, the rich found themselves threatened by new forms of taxation aimed at redistributing their wealth. Conspicuous consumption in the grand manner became dangerous, so highest prestige now once again goes to those who have most but show least. With the most prestigious members of the upper class no longer flaunting their wealth, some of the pressure on the middle class to engage in conspicuous consumption has also been removed. This suggests to me that the wearing of torn jeans and the rejection of overt consumerism among middle-class youth of late has more to do with aping the trends set by the upper class than with any so-called cultural revolution.

One final point. As I have shown, the replacement of reciprocity by competitive status seeking made it possible for larger human populations to survive and prosper in a given region. One might very well wish to question the sanity of the whole process by which mankind was tricked and cajoled into working harder in order to feed more people at substantially the same or even lower levels of material well-being than that enjoyed by people like the Eskimo or Bushmen. The only answer that I see to such a challenge is that many primitive societies refused to expand their productive effort and failed to increase their population density precisely because they discovered that the new "labor-saving" technologies actually meant that they would have to work harder as well as suffer a loss in living standards. But the fate of these primitive people was sealed as soon as any one of them —no matter how remotely situated—crossed the threshold to redistribution and the full-scale stratification of classes that lay beyond. Virtually all of the reciprocity-type hunters and gatherers were destroyed or forced into remote areas by bigger and more powerful societies that maximized production and population and that were organized by governing classes. At bottom, this replacement was essentially a matter of the ability of larger, denser, and better-organized societies to defeat simple hunters and gatherers in armed conflict. It was work hard or perish.

Phantom Cargo

I HAVE CHOSEN to tell you about phantom cargo at this point because it is directly related to redistributive exchange and the big-man system. You may not see the connection right away. But then nothing about phantom cargo is apparent right away.

The scene is a jungle airstrip high in the mountains of New Guinea. Nearby are thatch-roofed hangars, a radio shack, and a beacon tower made of bamboo. On the ground is an airplane made of sticks and leaves. The airstrip is manned twenty-four hours a day by a group of natives wearing nose ornaments and shell armbands. At night they keep a bonfire going to serve as a beacon. They are expecting the arrival of an important flight: cargo planes filled with canned food, clothing, portable radios, wrist watches, and motorcycles. The planes will be piloted by ancestors who have come back to life. Why the delay? A man goes inside the radio shack and gives instructions into the tin-can microphone. The message goes out over an antenna constructed of string and vines: "Do you read me? Roger and out." From time to time they watch a jet trail crossing the sky; occasionally they hear the sound of distant motors. The ancestors are overhead! They are looking for them. But the whites in the towns below are also sending messages. The ancestors are confused. They land at the wrong airport.

Waiting for ships or planes to bring dead ancestors and cargo began a long time ago. In the earliest cults the coastal people watched for a big canoe. Later, they watched for sails. In 1919 cult leaders searched the horizon for traces of smoke from steamships. After World War II, ancestors were expected in LST's, troop carriers, and Liberator bombers. Now they're coming in "flying houses" that rise higher than airplanes.

The cargo itself has also undergone modernization. In the earliest days, matches, steel tools, and bolts of calico accounted for most of the phantom cargo. Later, it was sacks of rice, shoes, canned meat and sardines, rifles, knives, ammunition, and tobacco. Recently, phantom fleets have been carrying automobiles, radios, and motorcycles. Some West Irian cargo prophets are predicting steamships that will disgorge whole factories and steel mills.

A precise inventory of cargo would be misleading. The natives are waiting for a total upgrading of their lives. The phantom ships and planes will bring the beginning of a whole new epoch. The dead and living will be reunited, the white man thrown out or subordinated, drudgery abolished; there will be no shortages of anything. The arrival of the cargo, in other words, will mark the beginning of heaven on earth. This vision differs from Western descriptions of the millennium only because of the bizarre prominence of industrial products. Jet planes and ancestors; motorcycles and miracles; radios and ghosts. Our own traditions prepare us for salvation, resurrection, immortality—but with airplanes, cars, and radios? No phantom ships for us. We know where such things come from. Or do we?

Missionaries and government administrators tell the natives that hard work and machines make the cornucopias of industrialism release their rivers of wealth. But the prophets of cargo hold to other theories. They insist that the material wealth of the industrial age is really created in some distant place not by human but by supernatural means. Missionaries, traders, and government officials know how to get consignments of this wealth sent to them by plane or ship—they possess the "secret of cargo." Native cargo prophets rise or fall on their ability to penetrate this secret and to deliver cargo into the hands of their followers.

Native theories about cargo evolve in response to continually changing conditions. Before World War II, ancestors had white skins; later they were said to look like Japanese; but when black American troops drove out the Japanese, ancestors were pictured as having black skins.

After World War II, cargo theory often centered on the Americans. In the New Hebrides, the people decided that a G.I. named John Frum was King of America. His prophets built an airport at which American Liberator bombers would land with a cargo of milk and ice cream. Relics left over on Pacific island battlefields show that John Frum was there. One group believes that a U.S. Army field jacket with sergeant's stripes and the red cross of the medical corps on the sleeves was worn by John Frum when he made his promise to return with cargo. Small medical corps red crosses, each surrounded by a neat fence, have been erected all over the island of Tanna. A John Frum village chieftain interviewed in 1970 noted that "people have waited nearly 2,000 years for Christ to return, so we can wait a while longer for John Frum."

During 1968, a prophet on the island of New Hanover in the Bismarck Archipelago announced that the secret of cargo was known only to the President of the United States. Refusing to pay local taxes, the cult members saved $75,000 to "buy" Lyndon Johnson and to make him King of New Hanover if he would tell the secret.

In 1962 the United States Air Force placed a large concrete survey marker on the top of Mt. Turu near Wewak, New Guinea. The prophet, Yaliwan Mathias, became convinced that the Americans were ancestors and that the cargo lay underneath the marker. In May 1971, after a night of prayer to the accompaniment of pop music on their transistor radio, he and his followers dug up the marker. No cargo was found. Yaliwan explained that the authorities had taken it away. His followers, who had contributed $21,500, did not lose faith.

It is easy to dismiss cargo beliefs as the ravings of primitive minds: Prophet leaders are either consummate rogues preying upon the greed, ignorance, and gullibility of their brethren, or if sincere, they are psychopaths who spread their mad ideas about cargo through autohypnosis and mass hysteria. This would be a cogent theory if there were nothing mysterious about how industrial wealth gets manufactured and distributed. But in point of fact, it is not easy to explain why some countries are poor and others rich, nor is it easy to say why there are such sharp differences in the distribution of wealth within modern nations. What I'm suggesting is that there really is a cargo mystery, and that the natives are justified in trying to solve it.

To penetrate the secret of cargo, we need to concentrate on a particular case. I have chosen the cults of the Madang area of the north coast of Australian New Guinea, which have been described by Peter Lawrence in his book *Road Belong Cargo*.

One of the first Europeans to visit the Madang coast was a nineteenth-century Russian explorer named Miklouho-Maclay. As soon as the boat landed, his men began to dispense steel axes, bolts of cloth, and other valuables as gifts. The natives decided that the white men were ancestors. The Europeans deliberately cultivated this image by never letting the natives witness the death of a white man—they would secretly dispose of the bodies at sea and explain that the missing men had gone back to heaven.

In 1884 Germany set up the first colonial government in Madang. Lutheran missionaries followed shortly, but they were unsuccessful in attracting converts. One mission went thirteen years without baptizing a single native. Converts had to be bribed with steel tools and food. And now you can see why I said that the concept of the big man is relevant. Like the native big men described in the last chapter, the big men from overseas remained credible and legitimate only to the extent that they held repeated giveaways. It made no difference whether they were returned ancestors or gods, except that godlike big men ought to give away more than ordinary big men. Hymn singing and the promise of future salvation were not enough to keep the natives interested. They wanted and expected cargo—everything the missionaries and their friends received by ship from the lands across the sea.

Big men, as we have seen, must redistribute their wealth. The natives believe that there is nothing worse than a stingy big man. The missionaries were clearly holding back—keeping the "meat and fat" for themselves and giving away the "bones and stale cakes." At the mission stations, on the road gangs, and on the plantation the natives worked hard, anticipating a great feast. Why didn't it come? In 1904 the natives plotted to kill all the stingy big men, but the authorities learned of the plot and executed the ringleaders. Martial law followed.

After this defeat, native intellectuals began to develop new theories about the orgin of cargo. Native ancestors, not Europeans, made cargo. But the Europeans were preventing the natives from getting their share. A second armed revolt was plotted in 1912. Then came the outbreak of World War I. The German big men fled and Australian big men took over.

The natives now held meetings at which they agreed that further armed resistance was impractical. Obviously the missionaries knew the secret of cargo. So the only thing to do was to learn it from them. The natives flocked to the churches and mission schools and became cooperative and enthusiastic Christians. They listened attentively to the following story: In the beginning God, called Anus in native mythology, created Heaven and Earth. Anus gave Adam and Eve a paradise full of cargo: all the canned meats, steel tools, rice in bags, and matches they could use. When Adam and Eve discovered sex, Anus took the cargo away from them and sent the flood. Anus showed Noah how to build a huge wooden steamship and made him its captain. Shem and Japheth obeyed Noah, their father. But Ham was stupid and disobeyed him. Noah took the cargo away from Ham and sent him to New Guinea. After they had lived for years in ignorance and darkness, Anus took pity on the children of Ham and sent the missionaries to undo Ham's mistake, saying: "You must win over his descendants to my ways again. When they follow me again, I shall send them cargo in the same way as I send it to you white men now."

The government and the missions were encouraged by the upturn in church attendance and the respectful sobriety of the new converts. Few whites comprehended the extent to which the native interpretation of Christianity deviated from their own. Sermons were conducted in Pidgin, a composite of German, English, and aboriginal languages. The missionaries knew that the natives took the phrase "and God blessed Noah," to mean "and God gave Noah cargo." And they knew that when they sermonized from Matthew "Seek ye first the kingdom of God, and his righteousness; and all these things shall be added unto you," the natives understood the passage to mean "Good Christians will be rewarded with cargo." But they also knew that if the rewards for Christian obedience were presented in a wholly spiritual and other-worldly sense, the natives would either disbelieve them or lose interest and move on to someone else's church. To the intelligent native, the message was loud and clear: Jesus and the ancestors were going to give cargo to the faithful; pagans would not only get no cargo, but they would burn in Hell. So during the twenties the native leaders patiently attended to their Christian duties—sang hymns, worked for a few cents an hour, paid their head tax, gave up their extra wives, and showed respect to the white bosses. But by the thirties their patience had begun to wear thin. If hard work brought cargo, they should already have gotten it. They had unloaded countless ships and planes for their white masters, but no native had ever received a single package from overseas.

The catechists and mission assistants were especially annoyed. They observed at first hand the substantial differences in wealth between themselves and the European big men. And they observed the patent failure of these differences to diminish as a result of all the effort expended on getting more converts and being good Christians. A prominent Lutheran minister, Rolland Hanselmann, entered his church one Sunday morning in 1933 and found all his native helpers standing behind a rope they had strung across the aisle. They read him a petition: "Why do we not learn the secret of the cargo? Christianity does not help us blackfellows in a practical way. The white men are hiding the cargo secret." There were additional accusations: the Bible was not translated properly by accident or design—it was being censored; the first page was missing; the true name of God was being withheld.

The natives boycotted the missions and put forward a new solution to the cargo mystery. Jesus Christ gave cargo to the Europeans. Now he wanted to give it to the natives. But the Jews and the missionaries had conspired to keep cargo for themselves. The Jews had captured Jesus and were holding him prisoner in or above Sydney, Australia. But soon Jesus would get free and cargo would start coming. The poorest would get the most ("the meek shall inherit"). The people stopped work, slaughtered their pigs, burned their gardens, and massed in the cemeteries.

These events coincided with the outbreak of World War II. At first, the natives had no trouble in understanding this new war. The Australians had driven out the Germans and now the Germans were going to drive out the Australians. Only this time the Germans would be ancestors disguised as German soldiers. The government jailed the cult leaders for spreading German propaganda. But despite a news blackout, the natives soon began to realize that their Australian administration was in danger of being driven out of New Guinea, not by the Germans, but by the Japanese.

The cargo prophets struggled to make sense out of this startling new development. A cult leader named Tagarab announced that the missionaries had been tricking them all along. Jesus was an unimportant god. The real God—the cargo god—was a native deity known as Kilibob. The missionaries had made the natives pray to Anus. But Anus was an ordinary human being who happened to be the father of Kilibob, who in turn was the father of Jesus. Kilibob was about to punish the whites for their perfidy. He and the ancestors were on their way with a shipload of guns, ammunition, and other military equipment. When they landed they would look like Japanese soldiers. The Australians would be driven out and everyone would get cargo. To get ready, everyone must cease ordinary work, slaughter pigs and chickens, and start building storehouses for the cargo.

When the Japanese finally invaded Madang in December 1942, the natives greeted them as liberators. Even though the Japanese had not brought cargo, the prophets interpreted their arrival as at least a partial fulfillment of cargo prophecies. The Japanese did not attempt to disabuse them. They gave the natives the impression that cargo had been tem-

141

porarily delayed because the fighting was still going on. They said that after the war was over, Madang was going to be part of Japan's Greater East Asia Co-Prosperity Sphere. Everyone would share in the good life to come. In the meantime there was work to be done; the natives were needed to help defeat the Australians and their American allies. The natives rushed to help unload the ships and planes; they acted as bearers, and brought gifts of fresh vegetables. Downed American pilots were unpleasantly surprised by the hostility displayed to them in the bush. No sooner did they touch ground than they were surrounded by painted tribesmen who tied their hands and feet, slung them on poles, and trotted off with them to the nearest Japanese officer. The Japanese rewarded the cargo prophets by presenting them with Samurai swords and making them officers in the local police force.

But tides of war soon brought this euphoric interval to a close. The Australians and Americans gained the initiative and cut the Japanese supply lines. As their military situation deteriorated, the Japanese stopped paying for food or labor. When Tagarab, wearing his Samurai sword, protested, he was shot. The "ancestors" began to strip the native gardens, coconut groves, and banana and sugar-cane plantations. They stole every last chicken and pig. When these were all gone, they fell upon the dogs and ate them. And when the dogs were gone, they hunted down the natives and ate them, too.

The Australians who retook Madang in April 1944 found the natives sullen and uncooperative. In a few areas where the Japanese had not been especially active, cargo prophets were already predicting the return of the Japanese in greater numbers than ever before. To gain the loyalty of the rest of the population the Australians began to talk about "development" in the postwar period. Native leaders were told that in the peace to come, blacks and whites would live together in harmony. Everyone was going to get decent housing, electricity, motor vehicles, boats, good clothing, and plenty of food.

By this time, the most worldly and intelligent of the native leaders were convinced that the missionaries were unmitigated liars. The prophet Yali, whose career I shall follow from now on, was especially adamant on this point. Yali had remained loyal to the Australians during the war and was rewarded with the rank of sergeant major in the Australian Army. He was taken to Australia and shown what the Australians wanted him to believe was the secret of cargo: sugar mills, breweries, an aircraft repair shop, and harbor warehouses. While Yali could now see for himself certain aspects of the production process, he could also see that not everyone driving about in cars and living in big houses worked in mills and breweries. He could see men and women working in organized groups, but he couldn't grasp the ultimate principles upon which their labor was organized. Nothing that he saw helped him to understand why from that vast outpouring of wealth, not even a trickle reached his fellow natives back home.

What impressed Yali most were not the roads, the lights, and the tall buildings, but the Queensland Museum and the Brisbane Zoo. To his amazement, the museum was full of native New Guinea artifacts. One of the exhibits even contained his own people's carved ceremonial mask worn in the great puberty rituals of former times—the very same mask

143

which the missionaries had called the "works of Satan." Now, carefully preserved behind glass, the mask was being worshiped by priests in white frocks and a steady stream of well-dressed visitors, who talked in hushed tones. The museum also contained glass cases in which some strange varieties of animal bones were being carefully preserved. In Brisbane, Yali was taken to the zoo, and there he saw the whites feeding and caring for more strange animals. Reaching Sydney, Yali paid careful attention to the number of dogs and cats people kept as pets.

It was not until after the war, while attending a government conference in Port Moresby, the capital of Australian New Guinea, that Yali realized the extent to which the missionaries had been lying to the natives. During the course of the conference Yali was shown a certain book which contained pictures of apes and monkeys becoming progressively more similar to men. At last the truth dawned on him: The missionaries had said that Adam and Eve were man's ancestors, but the whites really believed their own ancestors were monkeys, dogs, cats, and other animals. These were precisely the beliefs that the natives had possessed until the missionaries had tricked them into giving up their totems.

Later, in discussing his experiences with the prophet Gurek, Yali accepted the suggestion that the Queensland Museum was actually Rome, the place to which the missionaries had taken the New Guinea gods and myths in order to gain control over the secret of cargo. If these old gods and goddesses could be lured back to New Guinea, a new era of prosperity would dawn. But first they would have to abandon Christianity and revive their pagan ceremonies.

Yali was outraged by the duplicity of the missionaries. He

was willing and eager to help the Australian officials stamp out all vestiges of cargo cults in which God or Jesus had any importance. Because of Yali's war service, his familiarity with Brisbane and Sydney, and his eloquent denunciation of the cults, the district officer of Madang supposed that Yali didn't believe in cargo. Yali was asked to address mass meetings called by the government. He enthusiastically ridiculed the Christian cargo cults and assured everyone that cargo would never come unless people worked hard and obeyed the law.

Yali was also willing to collaborate with the Australian officials because he had not yet lost faith in the promises made to him while he was in the army during the war. Yali treasured the words uttered by a Brisbane recruiting officer in 1943: "In the past, you natives have been kept backward, but now if you help us win the war and get rid of the Japanese, we Europeans will help you. We will help you get houses with galvanized iron roofs, plank walls, electric lights, and motor vehicles, boats, good clothes, and good food. Life will be very different for you after the war."

Thousands came to hear Yali denounce the old road to cargo. Provided with a platform and loudspeakers, and surrounded by beaming officials and white businessmen, Yali warmed to his task. The more he denounced the former cargo beliefs, the more the natives understood him to be saying that he, Yali, knew the true secret of cargo. When word of this interpretation got back to Yali's "handlers" in the government, they demanded that he give more speeches to tell the natives that he was not a returned ancestor, and that he didn't know the secret of cargo. These public denials convinced the natives that Yali had supernatural powers and would bring cargo.

When Yali was invited to Port Moresby, along with other loyal native spokesmen, his followers in Madang believed that he would return at the head of a huge fleet of cargo ships. Yali himself may have believed that some important concessions were about to be made to him. He went straight to the administrator in charge and asked him when the natives were going to get the reward which the officer in Brisbane had promised. When would they get the building materials and machinery that everyone was talking about? Professor Lawrence's account of the official's reply to Yali is in *Road Belong Cargo.*

The officer is alleged to have replied that the administration was, of course, grateful for the services of native troops against the Japanese and was, in fact, going to give the people a substantial reward. The Australian Government was pouring vast sums of money into economic, educational, and political development, War Damage compensation, and schemes to improve medical services, hygiene and health. It would be a slow process, of course, but eventually the people would appreciate the results of the administration's efforts. But a reward of the nature Yali imagined—a free hand-out of cargo in bulk—was quite out of the question. The officer was sorry, but this was just wartime propaganda made by irresponsible European officers on the spur of the moment.

To questions about when natives could expect electricity, the administrators replied that they would get it as soon as they were able to pay for it and not before. Yali became very bitter. The government had lied as badly as the missionaries.

Upon his return from Port Moresby, Yali entered into a

secret alliance with the cargo prophet Gurek. Under Yali's protection, Gurek spread the word that the New Guinea deities, not the Christian deities, were the true source of cargo. The natives must abandon Christianity and go back to their pagan practices in order to acquire wealth and happiness. Traditional rituals and artifacts as well as pig husbandry and hunting were to be reintroduced. Male initiation ceremonies were to be performed. In addition, small tables were to be set up, covered with cotton cloth and decorated with bottles filled with flowers. At these shrines (inspired by domestic scenes glimpsed in Australian households), offerings of food and tobacco would induce the pagan deities and the ancestors to send cargo. The ancestors would bring rifles, ammunition, military equipment, horses, and cows. Yali was henceforth to be addressed as King, and Thursday, the day of Yali's birth, was to replace Sunday as the natives' Sabbath. Gurek said that Yali could perform miracles, and that he could kill people by spitting at them or cursing them.

Yali himself was repeatedly ordered out on patrol to put down the Yali cultists. He used these opportunities to suppress rival prophets and to establish a far-flung network of his own "boss boys" in the villages. He imposed fines and punishments, recruited labor, and maintained his own police force. Yali financed his organization by a clandestine system of redistribution. He promised to be a real big man.

The missionaries kept goading the administrators to get rid of Yali, but they found it hard to prove that he was actually behind the increasingly insolent behavior of the natives. It was even difficult to prove that there was a cargo cult, because the Yali cult members were all instructed to swear that they had no cargo beliefs. The natives were told that if they dared to reveal their cargo activities, the Europeans would steal the New Guinea gods for themselves once again. If the natives were asked about the table and flowers they were to answer that they were merely hoping to beautify their homes like the Europeans do. Whenever Yali was accused of stirring up trouble, he protested that he had nothing to do with the extremists in the villages who misrepresented his own publicly stated convictions.

Before long the Australian government was faced with what it regarded as an open rebellion. In 1950 Yali was arrested and tried on charges of incitement to rape and deprivation of the liberty of others. He was convicted and sentenced to six years in jail. Yali's career did not end, however. Even while he was in jail, Yali cult members kept scanning the horizon, awaiting his triumphant return at the head of a fleet of merchantmen and warships. During the sixties a number of political and economic concessions were finally made to the native peoples of New Guinea. Yali's followers gave him credit for the stepped-up rate of school construction, the opening of the legislative councils to native candidates, increased wages, and the end of the prohibition on the consumption of alcoholic beverages.

After his release from jail, Yali decided that the secret of the cargo lay in the New Guinea House of Assembly. He tried to get elected to the Madang Council but was defeated. As an old man he became the object of great veneration. "Flower girls" visited him once a year and brought away his semen in bottles. People continued to give him gifts, and he collected a fee for baptizing Christians who wanted to wash away the sins of Christianity and return to paganism.

Yali's last prophecy was that New Guinea would achieve independence on August 1, 1969. He prepared for this occasion by appointing ambassadors to Japan, China, and the United States.

Any human activity will appear inscrutable if it is jigsawed into snippets too small to be related to the overall historical picture. Viewed over a trajectory of appropriate length, cargo shows itself to be the working-out along lines of least resistance of a stubborn lopsided conflict. Cargo was the prize in the struggle for the natural and human resources of an island continent. Each snippet of savage mysticism matched a snippet of civilized rapacity, and the whole was firmly grounded in solid rewards and punishments rather than phantoms.

Like other groups, savage and civilized, whose dominions and freedom are threatened by invaders, the people of Madang tried to make the Europeans go home. Not at the very beginning, because several years elapsed before the invaders displayed their insatiable appetite for virgin lands and cheap native labor. Nonetheless, the attempt to kill off the enemy was not long in coming. It was doomed to failure because, as in so many other chapters of colonial warfare, the contending forces were drastically ill-matched. The Madang natives suffered from two insuperable handicaps: They lacked modern weapons, and they were fragmented into hundreds of tribelets and villages incapable of uniting against a common enemy.

The hope of using force to drive the Europeans away never quite disappeared; it was repressed, but not extinguished. The natives backed off, and came forward again

149

along what seem like crazy tangents. The invaders were treated like arrogant big men—too powerful to be destroyed, but still perhaps not invulnerable to manipulation. To get these strange big men to share more of their wealth and to moderate their appetite for land and labor, the natives tried to learn their language and penetrate their secrets. And so began the period of Christian conversion, abandonment of native customs, and submission to taxes and labor conscription. The natives learned "respect" and collaborated in their own exploitation.

This interval had consequences intended and foreseen by neither party. Separate and formerly hostile tribes and villages came together to serve the same master. They united in the belief that Christian big men could be manipulated into creating a state of paradisiacal redemption for all. They insisted that cargo be redistributed. This was not what the missionaries meant by Christianity. But the natives acted in their own self-interest in refusing to let Christianity mean what the missionaries wanted it to mean. They insisted on making the Europeans act like true big men; they insisted that those who possessed wealth were under the obligation to give it away.

Westerners are impressed by the natives' amusing inability to understand European economic and religious lifestyles. The implication is always that natives are too backward, stupid, or superstitious to grasp the principles of civilization. This certainly misrepresents the facts in Yali's case. It was not that Yali couldn't grasp the principles in question, but rather that he found them unacceptable. His tutors were amazed that someone who had seen modern factories in operation could still believe in cargo. But the more Yali learned about how Europeans produced wealth, the less was he prepared to accept their explanation of why he and his people were unable to share in it. This doesn't mean that he understood how the Europeans got to be so wealthy. On the contrary, when last heard from he was working on the theory that the Europeans had gotten rich by building brothels. But Yali always had the good sense to dismiss the standard European explanation, "hard work," as a calculated deception. Anyone could see that the European big men—unlike their native prototypes—scarcely worked at all.

Yali's understanding of the cosmos was scarcely a monopoly of the savage mind. In the South Seas, as in other colonial areas, the Christian missions enjoyed a virtually unchallenged mandate to provide the natives with an education. These missions were not about to disseminate the intellectual tools of political analysis; they did not offer instruction in the theory of European capitalism, nor did they embark upon an analysis of colonial economic policy. Instead they taught about creation, prophets and prophecies, angels, a messiah, supernatural redemption, resurrection, and an eternal kingdom in which the dead and the living would be reunited in a land of milk and honey.

Inevitably, these concepts—many rather precisely analogous to themes in the aboriginal belief system—had to become the idiom in which mass resistance to colonial exploitation was first expressed. "Mission Christianity" was the womb of rebellion. By repressing any form of open agitation, strikes, unions, or political parties, the Europeans themselves guaranteed the triumph of cargo. It was relatively easy to see that the missionaries were lying when they said that cargo would only be given to people who worked hard. What was difficult to grasp was that there was a definite link between the wealth enjoyed by the Australians and Americans and the work of the natives. Without the cheapness of native labor and the expropriation of native lands, the colonial powers would never have gotten so rich. In one sense, therefore, the natives were entitled to the products of the industrialized nations even though they couldn't pay for them. Cargo was their way of saying this. And that, I believe, is its true secret.

Messiahs

I'M SURE THAT you've noticed the resemblances between cargo cults and early Christian beliefs. Jesus of Nazareth predicted the downfall of the wicked, justice for the poor, the end of misery and suffering, reunion with the dead, and a whole new divine kingdom. So did Yali. Can the phantom cargo mystery help us to understand the conditions responsible for the origin of our own religious lifestyles?

There seem to be some important differences. The cargo cults were dedicated to the overthrow of a specific established political order and the creation of a kingdom which would have a definite terrestrial locus. The natives expected the dead to come to life as uniformed soldiers carrying weapons into battle against policemen and troops stationed in New Guinea. Jesus of Nazareth was not interested in the overthrow of any specific political system; he was above politics, his kingdom being "not of this world." When the first Christians spoke of "battles" against the wicked, their "swords," "fires," and "victories" were mere earthbound metaphors for transcendental spiritual events. At least that is what almost everybody believes the original Jesus cult was all about.

It seems impossible that a lifestyle so otherworldly in design, so devoted to peace, love, and selflessness, could have been in any fundamental sense a product of definite material conditions. Yet this riddle, like all the others, has its solution in the practical affairs of peoples and nations.

Actually two riddles need to be considered. Christianity arose first among Jews living in Palestine. Belief in the coming of a savior called a *messiah*—a god who would look like a man—was an important feature of Judaism at the time of Christ. The earliest followers of Jesus, almost all of whom were Jewish, believed that Jesus was this savior. ("Christ" is derived from *krystos*, which was the way Jews referred to their hoped-for savior when speaking Greek.) To solve the riddle of the early Christian lifestyle, I shall first have to explain the basis of the Jewish belief in a messiah.

All ancient peoples—not unlike most modern ones— believed that battles could not be won without divine assistance. To win an empire, or merely to survive as an independent state, you needed warriors with whom ancestors, angels, or gods were willing to cooperate.

David, the founder of the first and largest Jewish empire, claimed to be in divine partnership with the Jewish God, Jahweh. The people called David *messiah* (Hebrew: *mashia*), a term which they also applied to priests, shields, David's predecessor Saul, and David's son Solomon. So *messiah* probably originally meant any person or thing possessing great holiness and sacred power. David was also called the Anointed One—the one who, by collaboration with Jahweh, was entitled to rule over Jahweh's earthly domains.

David was born Elhanan ben Jesse. The name David, meaning "great commander," was given to him to celebrate his victories on the battlefield. His rise to power from humble beginnings provided the basic inspiration—the life plan— for the ideal Jewish military-messianic career. He was born in Bethlehem and spent his youth as a shepherd. Later, he became the outlaw leader of a guerrilla movement in the Judean desert. He located his headquarters in a cave and achieved his victories against seemingly insuperable odds— epitomized in the fight against Goliath.

The Jewish priests insisted down to the time of Jesus that Jahweh had made a covenant with David. Jahweh had promised that David's dynasty would never end. But David's empire actually began to crumble shortly after his death. It disappeared temporarily when Nebuchadnezzar captured Jerusalem in 586 B.C. and deported large numbers of Jews to Babylonia. Afterwards the Jewish state resumed a pre- carious existence as the dependent client of one or another imperial power.

Jahweh told Moses: "Ye shall rule over many nations but they shall not rule over thee." Yet Jahweh's promised land was an unlikely spot from which to launch the conquest of the world. For one thing, it was a military thruway—the main corridor along which all the imperial armies of Asia, Africa, and Europe chased each other to and from Egypt. Before any indigenous imperial growth could take root in Palestine, it was stamped out by some million-footed monster of an army passing in one direction or the other. Egyptians,

Assyrians, Babylonians, Persians, Greeks, and Romans sallied back and forth through the holy land, often burning the same place twice before they yielded to the next in line.

These experiences placed a considerable strain on the credibility of Jahweh's sacred books and his remnant priesthood. Why had Jahweh permitted so many nations to become great while his chosen people were repeatedly conquered and enslaved? Why hadn't Jahweh kept his promise to David? This was the great mystery which the Jewish holy men and prophets kept trying to decipher.

Their answer: Jahweh had not kept his promise to David because the Jews had not kept theirs to Jahweh. The people had violated the sacred laws and had practiced impure rites. They had sinned; they were guilty; they had caused their own ruin. But Jahweh was a forgiving God and he would still keep his promise if the Jews, despite their punishment, continued to believe that he was the One True God. By realizing what they had done, by repenting and asking for forgiveness, the people could atone for their sin and Jahweh would reinstitute the contract, save them, redeem them, and make them greater than ever before. Mysteriously, when the atonement was complete—at a moment known only to Jahweh—his people would be avenged. Jahweh would send another military prince like David, messiah, anointed one, to destroy the enemy nations. Great battles would be fought; the whole earth would heave with the clash of armies and the fall of cities. It would be the end of one world and the beginning of another, for Jahweh would not have made the Jews wait and suffer had he not intended to give them a greater reward than any previously known by man. And so the Old Testament teems with the promises of the redemptive prophets—Isaiah, Jeremiah, Ezekiel, Micah, Zechariah, and others—all urging or sanctioning the adoption of a military-messianic lifestyle.

Isaiah speaks of a "wonderful counselor, mighty God, Everlasting Father, Prince of Peace" who will reign forever on the throne of David. This savior will tread the Assyrian down "like the mire of the streets"; reduce Babylon to a deserted city inhabited by owls, satyrs, and other "doleful creatures"; make the people of Moab "bald and beardless, reduce Damascus to a ruinous heap," and provoke Egypt into civil war, "everyone against his neighbor, city against city and kingdom against kingdom."

Jeremiah has Jahweh say: "In those days and in that time, will I cause the Branch of Righteousness to grow up unto David; and he shall execute Judgement and righteousness in the land." And then "the sword shall devour" the Egyptian "and it shall be satiate and made drunk with their blood." The Philistines "shall cry and all the inhabitants of the land shall howl." From Moab "a continual weeping will go up." Ammon will become "a desolate heap and her daughters shall be burned in fire." Edom will be a "desolation." In Damascus "the young men shall fall in her streets." Hazor will become "a dwelling for dragons." Elam is to be "consumed by the sword," and as for Babylon: "Come against her from the utmost border, open her storehouses; cast her up as heaps and destroy her utterly: let nothing of her be left."

The Book of Daniel—written about 165 B.C., when Palestine was ruled by Syrian Greeks—also speaks of military-messianic redemption by an anointed one, the Prince, leading to a great Jewish empire: "I saw in the night visions, and behold the Son of Man came with the clouds of heaven . . .

and there was given him dominion, and glory, and a kingdom, that all the peoples, nations and languages shall serve him . . . an everlasting dominion . . . [a] kingdom that shall not be destroyed."

What most people fail to realize about these vengeful prophecies is that they were made in conjunction with actual wars of liberation waged under the leadership of real-life military messiahs. These wars enjoyed popular support because they not only aimed at restoring the independence of the Jewish state, but also promised to eliminate economic and social inequities that foreign rule had exacerbated beyond endurance.

Like cargo, the cult of the vengeful messiah was born and continually re-created out of a struggle to overturn an exploitative system of political and economic colonialism. Only in this case, the natives—the Jews—were militarily more of a match for the conquerors, and they were led by literate soldier-prophets, who remembered a far-off time when the "ancestors" had controlled an empire of their own.

During the period of Roman rule, if any lifestyle can be said to have been preeminent in Palestine, it was that of the vengeful military messiah. Inspired by the model of David's triumph against Goliath and the promise of Jahweh's military-messianic redemption, Jewish guerrillas waged a prolonged struggle against the Roman administrators and the Roman army. The cult of the peaceful messiah—the lifestyle of Jesus and his followers—developed in the midst of this guerrilla war and in the very districts of Palestine that were the main centers of insurgent activity, seemingly in total contradiction to the tactics and strategies of the liberation forces.

The Christian gospels fail to expound or even mention Jesus' relationship to the Jewish liberation struggle. From the gospels alone, you would never know that Jesus spent most of his life in the central theater of one of history's fiercest guerrilla uprisings. Even less apparent to readers of the gospels is the fact that this struggle continued to escalate long after Jesus was executed. You could never guess that in 68 A.D. the Jews went on to stage a full-scale revolution that required the attention of six Roman legions under the command of two future Roman emperors before it was brought under control. And least of all would you ever suspect that Jesus himself died a victim of the Roman attempt to destroy the military-messianic consciousness of the Jewish revolutionaries.

As a Roman colony, Palestine exhibited all of the classical political and economic symptoms of colonial misrule. The Jews who occupied high civil or religious positions were puppets or clients. The high priests, wealthy landowners, and merchants lived in Oriental splendor, but the bulk of the population consisted of landless, alienated peasants, poorly paid or unemployed artisans, servants, and slaves. The country groaned under the weight of confiscatory taxes, administrative corruption, arbitrary tribute, labor conscription, and runaway inflation. Absentee landlords lived in pomp in Jerusalem while their tenants absorbed the 25 percent tax which the Romans imposed on agricultural production, on top of a 22 percent tax on the remainder claimed by the temple. The hatred of the Galilean peasants for the Jerusalem aristocrats was especially glaring and openly reciprocated. In the Talmudic commentaries, true Jews are advised not to let their daughters marry the "people of the land," as the Galilean peasants were called, "because they are unclean animals." Rabbi Eleazar sarcastically recommended the butchering of these types even on the most holy day of the year, when no animals may be killed; and Rabbi Joahanan said, "One may tear a common person to pieces like a fish," while Rabbi Eleazar said, "The enmity of a common person toward a scholar is even more intense than that of the heathen toward the Israelites."

Popular enthusiasm for the military-messianic ideal went beyond a desire to see Jewish nationalists replace foreign puppets. The Galileans wanted to see David's kingdom restored because the prophets said that the messiah would end economic and social exploitation and punish the wicked priests, landlords, and kings. This theme was announced in the Book of Enoch:

Woe to you, ye rich, for ye have trusted in your riches and from your riches ye shall be torn away.... Woe to you who requite your neighbor with evil, for you will be requited according to your works. Woe to you, ye lying witnesses.... But fear not, ye that suffer, for healing will be your portion.

The dialectic of Jahweh's kingdom necessarily embraced the totality of human experience. As in the case of cargo, secular and sacred components were indivisible; "this-worldly" and otherworldly themes were inseparable. Politics, religion, and economics were fused; heaven and earth were confounded, nature was married to God. In the new universe, life would be completely different; everything would be turned upside down. The Jews would rule and the Romans serve. The poor would be rich, the wicked would be punished, the sick would be healed, and the dead brought to life.

The Jews began their war against Rome shortly before Herod the Great was confirmed as puppet king by the Roman Senate. At first, guerrillas were identified by the Romans and the Jewish ruling class merely as bandits (Greek: *lestai*). But these bandits were not so much guilty of thefts as of programs directed against the absentee landlords and the Roman tax collectors. The other term applied to the guerrilla fighters was "'zealots"—indicative of their zeal for the Jewish law and the fulfillment of Jahweh's covenant.

Neither term alone properly conveys the sense of what these activists were doing. It is only as zealot-bandits—guerrillas—that their exploits can be related to the everyday context of their world. The zealot-bandit-guerrillas believed that with the help of a messiah they would eventually be able to topple the Roman Empire. Their faith was not a state of mind; it was a revolutionary praxis involving harassment, provocation, robbery, assassination, terrorism, and acts of bravery ending in death. Some specialized in urban guerrilla tactics and were called "dagger men" (Latin: *sicarii*); the rest lived in the countryside, in caves and mountain hideouts, depending on the peasants for food and security.

Any description of the political and military events in Palestine during the first century A.D. has to be based largely upon the writings of one of the great historians of the ancient world, Flavius Josephus. Since the matters that I am about to discuss are likely to be unfamiliar, let me say a word about the reliability of this source. Josephus was a contemporary of the authors of the earliest Christian gospels. Two of his books, *The Jewish War* and *Jewish Antiquities*, are recognized by scholars as no less essential to the history of first-century Palestine than the gospels themselves. We have definite knowledge of who Josephus was and of how he came to write his books—knowledge which we do not have about the authors of the gospels. Josephus was born Joseph ben Matthias in 37 A.D., the child of an upper-class Jewish family. In 68 A.D., when he was only thirty-one years old, Josephus became governor of Galilee and a general in the Jewish liberation army in the war against Rome. After his followers were wiped out in the seige of Jotapata, Josephus surrendered and was brought before Vespasian, the Roman general, and Vespasian's son Titus. Josephus thereupon announced that Vespasian was the messiah the Jews had been awaiting and that both Vespasian and Titus would be future emperors of Rome.

Vespasian did in fact become emperor in 69 A.D., and as a reward for his prophetic words, Josephus was taken to Rome as part of the new emperor's entourage. He was given Roman citizenship, an apartment in the imperial palace, and a life pension based on income from farms which the Romans had confiscated as spoils of the war in Palestine.

Josephus spent the rest of his life writing books explaining why the Jews had revolted against Rome and why he himself had defected to the Roman side. Writing in Rome for Roman readers—many of whom, including the emperor, were eyewitnesses to the events described—Josephus was unlikely to have fabricated the basic facts of his history. The distortions that have been identified are related in obvious ways to Josephus' desire not to be labeled a traitor and can easily be discounted without impairing the credibility of the main narrative.

The events recounted by Josephus make it clear that guerrilla activism and the Jewish military-messianic consciousness rose and fell in synergetic waves. The dusty, sun-baked backlands were filled with wandering holy men, strangely dressed oracles who spoke in parables and allegories and made prophecies about the coming battle for world dominion. Successful guerrilla leaders inspired rumors that flourished in the light and shadow of these perennially renewed messianic speculations. A steady stream of charismatic leaders stepped forward into the glare of history to claim messiahship; at least two of them precipitated insurrections that actually shook the foundation of the Roman Empire.

Herod the Great first attracted the attention of his Roman patrons because he waged a vigorous campaign against a bandit chief who controlled an entire district in northern Galilee. According to Josephus, Herod trapped this bandit chief, whose name was Hezekiah, and executed him on the spot. But we know that Hezekiah was a guerrilla leader rather than an ordinary thief because the bandit's sympathizers in Jerusalem were powerful enough to force Herod to stand trial for murder. A cousin of Julius Caesar intervened, obtained Herod's release, and gave him the recommendation that soon led to Herod's appointment as puppet king of the Jews in 39 B.C.

Herod had to fight more bandits in order to consolidate his control over Palestine. Josephus declares that "bandits overran a great part of the country, causing the inhabitants as much misery as a war could have done." So Herod "took to the field against the bandits in the caves." When trapped inside, the bandits turned out to have their families with them, and they refused to surrender. One old bandit stood at the mouth of an inaccessible cave and in full sight of Herod killed his wife and each of his seven children "and went so far as to sneer at Herod" before leaping to his own death. Thinking himself "master now of caves and cave-dwellers," Herod left for Samaria. But his departure removed all restraint from the "habitual troublemakers in Galilee," who promptly killed a Roman general named Ptolemy and "systematically ravaged the country, establishing their lairs in the marshes and other inaccessible places."

Upon Herod's death in 4 B.C. uprisings took place in all outlying areas. Hezekiah's son, Judas of Galilee, seized a royal armory. Simultaneously in Peraea across the Jordan, a slave named Simon "burnt the palace at Jericho and many magnificent country residences." A third rebel, a former shepherd named Athrongaeus, "declared himself king"—which is probably Josephus' way of saying that he was considered a messiah by his followers. Before the Romans killed Athrongaeus and four of his brothers, one by one, these bandits succeeded in "harassing all Judea with their brigandage." Varus, the Roman governor of Syria, restored law and order. He captured 2,000 "ringleaders" and had them all crucified. This event occurred in the year that Jesus was born.

Judas of Galilee soon emerged as the leader of the main guerrilla forces. Josephus says he "aspired to royalty," and at times characterizes him as "a very clever rabbi." In 6 A.D. the Romans tried to carry out a census. Judas warned his countrymen to resist because the census would lead to "nothing less than complete slavery." Josephus has him say

Messiahs

that "the Jews have no king but Jahweh." Therefore "taxes should not be paid to the Romans" and "Jahweh would surely assist them if they had faith in their cause." Josephus reports that those prepared to submit to Rome were treated as enemies: Their cattle were rounded up and their dwellings burned.

No information has survived concerning how and when Judas of Galilee met his fate. We know only that his sons continued to fight. Two were crucified, and another claimed messiahship at the beginning of the revolution of 68–73. The final act of resistance in that war, the suicidal defense of the fortress of Masada, was led by still another descendant of Judas of Galilee.

Jesus actively began to preach his messianic doctrines about 28 A.D. At that time a "shooting war" was being fought, not only in Galilee, but in Judea and Jerusalem as well. The Jesus cult was neither the largest nor the most threatening of the rebellious situations with which Pontius Pilate, the Roman governor who decreed Jesus' death, had to contend. For example, Josephus describes the appearance of an angry city mob joined by a huge influx from the country when Pilate transgressed the Jewish taboo on graven images in Jerusalem. Later, Pilate was surrounded by another angry mob protesting the misuse of temple funds for the construction of an aqueduct. From the gospels we know that Jesus himself led an attack on the temple, and that some sort of uprising took place shortly before Jesus' trial, since the popular bandit leader Barabbas and several of his men were in jail at that point.

After Jesus was killed, the Romans continued to try to clear the Judean countryside of "bandits." Josephus reports that another great bandit chief named Tholomaios was captured in 44 A.D. Shortly thereafter, a messianic figure named Theudas appeared in the desert. His followers abandoned their homes and posessions and massed on the banks of the Jordan River. Some say Theudas intended to make the waters part as they had done for Joshua; others that this messiah was going the other way, westward, toward Jerusalem. No matter—the Roman governor Cuspius Fadus sent the cavalry; they beheaded Theudas and slaughtered his followers.

During the feast of Passover in 50 A.D. a Roman soldier pulled up his tunic and farted into a crowd of pilgrims and temple worshipers. "The less restrained of the young men and the naturally tumultuous segments of the people rushed into battle," writes Josephus. The Roman heavy infantry was called in, creating a gigantic panic in which, according to Josephus, 30,000 people were trampled to death (some say he probably meant 3,000). Jesus' attack on the temple had coincided with the Passover pilgrimage of 33 A.D. As we shall see, concern with the reaction of mobs of pilgrims like those who died in the panic of 50 A.D. led the Jewish and Roman authorities to wait until nightfall to take Jesus into custody.

Something close to a general revolt developed in 52 A.D. under the leadership of Eleazar ben Deinaios, a "revolutionary bandit" who had been in the mountains for almost twenty years. The governor, Cumanus, "rounded up Eleazar's followers, killing still more." But the disorder spread "and all over the country plundering went on and the bolder spirits rose in revolt." The Syrian Legate intervened, beheaded eighteen partisans, and crucified all of the prisoners who had been rounded up by Cumanus. The revolt was finally crushed by a new governor, Felix, who captured Eleazar and sent him to Rome—probably to be strangled in public. "The bandits whom he crucified," says Josephus, "and the local inhabitants in league with them whom he caught and punished were too many to count."

In Jerusalem, assassinations by dagger men who concealed their weapons inside their garments now had become common. One of their most famous victims was the High Priest Jonathan. In the midst of all this bloodshed, military-messianic contenders appeared again and again. Josephus refers to one set of messianic leaders as

scoundrels in act less criminal but in intention more evil, who did as much damage as the murderers—cheats and deceivers. Claiming inspiration, they schemed to bring about revolutionary changes by inducing the mob to act as if possessed, and by leading them out into the wild country on the pretense that there God would show them signs of approaching freedom.

Felix interpreted this foray as the first stage of a revolt and ordered the Roman cavalry to cut the mob to pieces.

Next came a Jewish Egyptian "false prophet." He collected several thousand "dupes," led them into the desert, then turned around and tried to attack Jerusalem—providing confirmation, if the Romans needed it, that all such people were politically dangerous. Josephus gives the following picture of the situation in Palestine about 55 A.D.:

The religious frauds and bandit chiefs joined forces and drove numbers to revolt. Splitting up into groups they ranged over the countryside, plundering the houses of the well-to-do, killing the occupants, and setting fire to the villages, till their raging madness penetrated every corner of Judea. Day by day the fighting blazed more fiercely.

By 66 A.D. the bandits were everywhere; their agents had infiltrated the temple priesthood and forged an alliance with Eleazar, the son of the High Priest Ananias. Eleazar issued a kind of declaration of independence: an order preventing the daily sacrifice of animals dedicated to the health of Nero, the reigning emperor. The pro-Roman and anti-Roman factions began to fight in the streets of Jerusalem: dagger men, freed slaves, and the Jerusalem rabble led by Eleazar on one side; the high priests, the Herodian aristocracy, and the Roman royal guard on the other.

Meanwhile, in the backlands, Manahem, the last surviving son of Judas of Galilee, stormed the fortress of Masada, equipped his bandits with Roman weapons taken from the armory, and marched on Jerusalem. Bursting onto a chaotic scene, Manahem took command of the insurrection—"like a king," says Josephus. He drove out the Roman troops, gained control of the temple area, and murdered the High Priest Ananias. Manahem then decked himself with kingly robes, and followed by a train of armed bandits, prepared to enter the sanctuary of the temple. But Eleazar, possibly to avenge his father's death, ambushed the cortege. Manahem fled but was captured and "put to death by prolonged torture."

The Jews fought on, convinced that the real messiah would yet appear. After the Romans had suffered several reverses, Nero called in his best general, Vespasian, veteran of the campaigns against the Britons. With 65,000 men and the most advanced forms of military engines and siegecraft, the Romans slowly regained control of the smaller cities.

On Nero's death in 68 A.D. Vespasian emerged as the favored candidate for emperor. Assured of all the men and equipment he might need, Vespasian's son Titus finished the war. Despite fanatic resistance, Titus broke into Jerusalem in 70 A.D., set fire to the temple, and looted and burned everything in sight.

Reflecting that the siege of Jerusalem had cost the Jews over one million casualties, Josephus bitterly denounced the messianic oracles. There had been terrible portents—bright lights on the altar, a cow that gave birth to a lamb, chariots and regiments in arms speeding through the sky at sunset—but the bandits and their execrable prophets missed these signs of doom. These "cheats and false messengers beguiled the people into believing that supernatural deliverance would yet be theirs."

Even after the fall of Jerusalem, the bandits still could not believe that Jahweh had deserted them. One more heroic effort—one more blood sacrifice—and Jahweh would at last decide to send the true anointed one. As I mentioned before, the last sacrifice took place at the fortress of Masada in 73 A.D. A bandit named Eleazar, descendant of Hezekiah and of Judas of Galilee, exhorted his remnant force of 960 men, women, and children to kill each other rather than surrender to the Romans.

To sum up: Between 40 B.C. and 73 A.D., Josephus mentions at least five Jewish military messiahs, not including Jesus or John the Baptist. These are Athrongaeus; Theudas; the anonymous "scoundrel" executed by Felix; the Jewish Egyptian "false prophet"; and Manahem. But Josephus repeatedly alludes to other messiahs or prophets of messiahs whom he does not bother to name or describe. In addition, it seems to me very likely that the entire lineage of zealot-bandit-guerrillas that descended from Hezekiah through Judas of Galilee, Manahem, and Eleazar were believed by many of their followers to be messiahs or prophets of messiahs. In other words, at the time of Jesus, there were as many messiahs in Palestine as there are today cargo prophets in the South Seas.

The fall of Masada was scarcely the end of the Jewish military-messianic lifestyle. Continuously re-created by the practical exigencies of colonialism and poverty, the revolutionary impulse burst forth again sixty years after Masada, in an even more spectacular messianic drama. In 132, Bar Kochva—"Son of a Star"—organized a force of 200,000 men and set up an independent Jewish state that endured for three years. Because of Bar Kochva's miraculous victories, Akiba, the chief rabbi of Jerusalem, hailed him as messiah. The people reported seeing Bar Kochva mounted on a lion. Not since Hannibal had the Romans faced a military opponent of such daring; he fought in the front ranks and at the most dangerous points. A whole Roman legion was lost before Bar Kochva was cut down. The Romans leveled 1,000 villages, killed 500,000 people, and shipped thousands more abroad as slaves. Generations of embittered Jewish scholars thereafter spoke ruefully of Bar Kochva as the "son of a lie" who had duped them into losing their homeland.

History shows that the Jewish military-messianic lifestyle was an adaptive failure. It did not succeed in restoring David's kingdom; rather, it resulted in the complete loss of the territorial integrity of the Jewish state. For the next eighteen hundred years the Jews were a subordinate minority no matter where they lived. Does this mean that military messianism was a capricious, impractical, even maniacal lifestyle? Are we to conclude along with Josephus and those who later condemned Bar Kochva that the Jews lost their homeland because they let the messianic will-o'-the-wisp dupe them into attacking the invincible power of Rome? I think not.

The Jewish revolution against Rome was caused by the inequities of Roman colonialism, not by Jewish military messianism. We cannot judge the Romans as more "practical" or "realistic" simply because they were the victors. Both sides went to war for practical and mundane reasons. Suppose George Washington had lost the American Revolutionary War. Would we then want to conclude that the Continental Army was the victim of an irrational lifestyle consciousness dedicated to the will-o'-the-wisp called "freedom"?

In culture, as in nature, systems that are the product of selective forces frequently fail to survive, not because they are defective or irrational, but because they encounter other systems that are better adapted and more powerful. I think I have shown that the cult of the vengeful messiah, like cargo, was adapted to the practical exigencies of a colonial struggle. It was extremely successful as a means of mobilizing mass resistance in the absence of a formal apparatus for raising and training an army. I would not judge the zealot-bandits to have been duped unless it can be shown that the probability of their defeat was so great at the outset that no amount of effort could ever have led to any result other than the one that history now reveals. But there is no way of proving that the zealot-bandits could have predicted that their defeat was inevitable. History reveals with equal finality that Judas of Galilee was right and the Caesars wrong about the alleged invincibility of the Roman Empire. The Roman Empire was not only eventually destroyed, but the people who destroyed it were colonials like the Jews, and vastly inferior to the Romans in numbers, equipment, and military skills.

Almost by definition, revolution means that an exploited population must take desperate measures against great odds to overthrow its oppressors. Classes, races, and nations usually accept the challenge of such odds not because they are duped by irrational ideologies, but because the alternatives are abhorrent enough to make even great risks worthwhile. That, I believe, is the reason the Jews revolted against Rome. And that is the reason why the Jewish military-messianic consciousness underwent a great expansion at the time of Christ.

To the extent that the cult of the vengeful messiah was rooted in the practical struggle against Roman colonialism, the cult of the peaceful messiah assumes the guise of an apparently inscrutable paradox. The peaceful messiah of Christendom came at a most improbable moment in the 180-year trajectory of the war against Rome. The Jesus cult developed while the military-messianic consciousness was still accelerating, expanding, soaring toward the untarnished ecstasy of Jahweh's grace. Its timing seems all wrong. In 30 A.D. no major obstacle to the zealot-bandit revolutionary impulse had yet been encountered. The temple was intact and was the scene of great annual pilgrimages. Judas of

Galilee's sons were alive. The terror of Masada was as yet unimagined. Why should the Jews have yearned for a peaceful messiah so many years before the military-messianic dream had anointed Manahem and Bar Kochva? Why surrender Palestine to the Roman overlords when Roman power had not so much as nicked the edge of Jahweh's sacred shield? Why a new covenant while the old one was still capable of twice shaking the Roman Empire?

The Secret of
the Prince of Peace

THE DREAMWORK of Western civilization is not fundamentally different from the dreamworks of other peoples. Only a knowledge of practical circumstances is needed to penetrate its mysteries.

In the case before us, there really are very few practical options to choose from. It would be most convenient if the dating of Jesus's ministry was wrong—if it could be shown that Jesus had not begun to urge his fellow Jews to love the Romans until after the fall of Jerusalem. But an error of forty years in the conventional chronology of events such as Judas of Galilee's tax revolt or Pontius Pilate's governorship is inconceivable.

Although we cannot be in error about *when* Jesus spoke, there are many reasons to suppose that we are in error about *what* he spoke. A simple practical solution to the questions raised at the close of the previous chapter is that Jesus was not as peaceful as is commonly believed, and that his actual teachings did not represent a fundamental break with the

179

tradition of Jewish military messianism. A strong pro-zealot-bandit and anti-Roman bias probably pervaded his original ministry. The decisive break with the Jewish messianic tradition probably came about only after the fall of Jerusalem, when the original politico-military components in Jesus' teachings were purged by Jewish Christians living in Rome and other cities of the empire as an adaptive response to the Roman victory. That, at least in brief, is the argument that I shall employ now in order to relate the paradoxes of peaceful messianism to the conduct of practical human affairs.

Continuity between the original teachings of Jesus and the military-messianic tradition is suggested by the close link that existed between Jesus and John the Baptist. Dressed in animal skins and eating nothing but locusts and wild honey, John the Baptist clearly corresponds to that genre of holy men whom Josephus describes as wandering about the badlands of the Jordan Valley, stirring up the peasants and slaves and making trouble for the Romans and their Jewish clients.

All four gospels agree that John the Baptist was the immediate forerunner of Jesus. His mission was to perform the work of Isaiah, to go into the wilderness—the bandit-infested backlands full of caves that echoed with the memories of Jahweh's covenant—and cry out: "Prepare ye the ways of the Lord; make his paths straight." (Repent for your sinfulness, recognize your guilt, so that you may at least be rewarded with the promised empire.) John "baptized" Jews who confessed their guilt and were properly penitent, bathing them in a river or spring to symbolically wash away their sins. According to the gospels, Jesus was the Baptist's most famous penitent. Upon being washed in the Jordan River, Jesus embarked on the climactic phase of his life—the period of active preaching that led to his death on the cross.

John the Baptist's career replicates the pattern of desert oracles described in the previous chapter. When the crowds around him grew too big, he was taken into custody by the nearest guardian of Roman law and order. This happened to be the puppet king, Herod Antipas, ruler of the part of Palestine east of the Jordan where the Baptist had been most active.

There is no hint in the gospels that John the Baptist might have been arrested because his activities were regarded as a threat to law and order. The entire politico-military dimension is absent. Instead we are told that John the Baptist's arrest resulted from his criticism of the marriage between Herod and Herodias, the divorced wife of one of Herod's brothers. The story goes on to attribute John the Baptist's execution not to any political motive but to Herodias's desire for revenge. Herodias gets her daughter Salome to dance for King Herod. The king is so pleased with the performance that he promises the dancer anything she wants. Salome announces she wants John the Baptist's head on a platter, and Herod complies. Herod is said to have been overcome with remorse, just as later on Pontius Pilate is said to have been overcome with remorse at the execution of Jesus. Considering what John the Baptist was telling the crowds in the wilderness before he was arrested, the lack of political references and the remorse attributed to Herod seem most inappropriate. What John preached was a pure military-messianic threat:

One mightier than I cometh—He shall baptize you in spirit and fire: his winnowing fan is in his hand, and he will thoroughly cleanse his threshing-floor, and gather the wheat into his barn; but the chaff he will burn up with unquenchable fire.

Was Herod Antipas blind to the connection between the desert oracles and the zealot-bandits? A king whose reign was to last forty-three years and who was the son of the tyrant bandit-killer Herod the Great could not have been indifferent to the dangers involved in permitting people like John the Baptist to attract large crowds in the desert. And how could an oracle whose messiah was not related to the zealot-bandit cause attract such large crowds?

The Baptist's place in the military-messianic tradition has been clarified as a result of the discovery of the Dead Sea Scrolls. These documents were found in a cave near the ruins of an ancient pre-Christian community called Quamran, located in the region where John baptized Jesus. Quamran itself was a religious commune dedicated, like John the Baptist, to "clearing the path in the wilderness." According to the commune's rich and previously unknown sacred literature, the history of the Jews was leading toward an Armageddon in which the Roman Empire would meet its doom. Rome was to be replaced by a new empire with its capital in Jerusalem, ruled over by a military messiah descended from a branch of the House of David, mightier than any Caesar yet seen on earth. Led by the "anointed one of Israel," invincible general, commander in chief, the Jewish "Sons of Light" were to go into battle against the Roman "Sons of Darkness." It would be a war of annihilation. Twenty-eight thousand Jewish warriors and six thousand charioteers were to strike against the Romans. They "will take up the pursuit in order to exterminate the enemy in an eternal annihilation . . . until he is wiped out." Victory was guaranteed because "as thou hast declared to us from old; 'a star shall come forth from Jacob, a sceptre shall rise from Israel'" (the prophecy in the Book of Numbers that was later applied to Bar Kochva). Israel was to be victorious "because as in the past, through thine anointed ones thou hast devoured evil like a blazing torch in a swath of grain . . . for of old thou hast proclaimed that the enemy . . . shall fall by a sword not of man, and a sword not of man shall devour him."

The Quamranites had the order of battle worked out down to the last detail. They were even ready with a song of victory:

> Arise, O Valiant One!
> Lead away Thy captives, O glorious Man!
> Do Thy plundering, O valorous One!
> Set Thy hand upon the neck of Thine enemies
> And Thy foot upon the heap of the slain!
> Strike the nations Thy enemies
> And let Thy sword devour guilty flesh!
> Fill the land with glory
> And Thine inheritance with blessing!
> A multitude of cattle in Thy pastures,
> Silver and gold and precious stones in thy palaces!
> O Zion, rejoice greatly!
> Appear amid shouts of joy, O Jerusalem!
> Show yourselves, O all you cities of Judah!
> Open thy gates forever.
> For the riches of the nations to enter in!
> And let their kings serve thee
> And let all thy oppressors bow down before thee
> And let them lick the dust of thy feet!

We know that the Quamranites sent missionaries to act as a vanguard for the Anointed One. Like John the Baptist, these missionaries are said to have eaten locusts and wild honey and dressed in the skins of animals. Like John the Baptist, their task was to make the children of Israel repent. It can't be proved that they also practiced baptism, but at Quamran itself archaeologists have uncovered extensive ritual bathing facilities. John's ritual of baptism may very well have been introduced as an abbreviated form of the more extensive ablutions and purificatory rites performed in the commune's baths and which in one form or another were long a part of Jewish ideas about spiritual cleanliness.

I think a point that needs special emphasis here is that the existence of this literature was not even hinted at in the writings of such people as Josephus or the authors of the Christian gospels. Without the scrolls we would know absolutely nothing about what these militant holy men were up to, because Quamran was destroyed by the Romans in 68 A.D. The communards sealed their sacred library in jars and hid them in nearby caves before the "Sons of Darkness" swooped down and obliterated the commune. Because they could not have been tampered with during the two thousand years their existence was forgotten, the scrolls now constitute one of the great manuscript sources of information about Judaism in the period immediately prior to, during, and shortly after the time of Christ.

The Quamran scrolls make it extremely difficult to separate John the Baptist's teachings as reported in the gospels from the mainstream of the Jewish military-messianic tradition. In the ambience of the prolonged and bloody guerrilla war with Rome, the Baptist's metaphor of "chaff burned in unquenchable fire" cannot reasonably be opposed to what the Quamranites predict about a "blazing torch in a swath of grain." I don't propose to say what was in John the Baptist's mind, but the earthly context in which his behavior should be judged can't be that of a religion as yet unborn. I can only think of his reported sayings and actions in the context of a dusty, surging ragtag mass of peasants, guerrillas, tax evaders, and thieves, knee-deep in the Jordan, burning with an unquenchable hatred for the Herodian tyrants, puppet priests, arrogant Roman governors, and heathen soldiers who farted in holy places.

Immediately after the Baptist was captured—probably while he was still awaiting trial in Herod Antipas' prison—Jesus began to preach among precisely the same kind of people and under the same kinds of risky conditions. The resemblance in lifestyle was so great that among Jesus' first disciples, at least two—the brothers Andrew and Simon Peter (St. Peter)—were former followers of the Baptist. Herod Antipas later found so little difference between Jesus and the Baptist that he is said to have remarked, "It is John, whom I beheaded; he is risen from the dead." At first Jesus did most of his preaching in the back country, performing miracles and attracting large crowds. He was probably always only one jump ahead of the police. Like John the Baptist and the messianic messengers discussed by Josephus, Jesus was launched on a collision course that would end either in his arrest or in a cataclysmic insurrection.

The logic of his growing popularity drew Jesus forward into increasingly dangerous exploits. Before long, he and his disciples set out to missionize Jerusalem, the promised capital of the future Holy Jewish Empire. Deliberately invoking the

messianic symbolism of the Book of Zechariah, Jesus rode
through the gates mounted on a donkey (or possibly a pony).
Sunday School teachers claim that Jesus did this because it
signified an intention to "speak peace unto the heathen." This
ignores the overwhelmingly military-messianic significance
of everything else in Zechariah. For after Zechariah's messiah appears, lowly and riding on an ass, the sons of Zion
"devour and subdue" . . . and become "mighty men which
tread down their enemies in the mire of the streets in battle
. . . because the Lord is with them and the riders on horses
shall be confounded."

The lowly figure on the ass was not a peaceful messiah. It
was the messiah of a small nation and its apparently harmless
prince of war, a descendant of David, who also rose from
apparent weakness to confound and subdue the enemy's
horsemen and charioteers. The heathen were to have peace—
but it was to be the peace of the long-awaited Holy Jewish
Empire. That at least is how the crowds who lined the way
understood what was happening, for as Jesus passed by, they
shouted: "Hosanna! Blessed is he that comes in the name
of the Lord! Blessed be the Kingdom of our Father David
that is coming!"

Nor was there anything notably peaceful in what Jesus
and his disciples did after they entered the city. By choosing
to invade Jerusalem just before the beginning of Passover,
they assured themselves the protection of thousands of holi-
day pilgrims arriving from the countryside and from all over
the Mediterranean. Zealot-bandits, peasants, laborers, beg-
gars and other potentially volatile groups were all streaming
into the city at the same time. During the day Jesus went
nowhere unless surrounded by tumultuous and ecstatic

crowds. When it became dark he slipped away to the houses of friends, keeping his whereabouts hidden from all but the inner core of disciples.

Jesus and his disciples did nothing that would have distinguished them from the members of an incipient military-messianic movement. They even provoked at least one violent confrontation. They stormed into the courtyard of the great temple and physically attacked the licensed business-men who changed currencies so that foreign pilgrims could purchase sacrificial animals. Jesus himself used a whip during this incident.

The gospels recount how Caiaphas, the High Priest, "plotted" to arrest Jesus. Since Caiaphas had witnessed the violent attack against the moneychangers, he could not have entertained any doubts about the legality of putting Jesus in jail. What Caiaphas had to figure out was how to arrest Jesus without provoking all the people who thought he was the messiah. Mobs were extremely dangerous in those days before the invention of shotguns and tear gas, especially if the people believed they had an invincible leader. So Caiaphas instructed the police to take Jesus, but "not on the feast day, lest there be an uproar of the people."

The crowd surrounding Jesus certainly had not had time to adopt a nonviolent lifestyle. Even his most intimate disciples were clearly not prepared to "turn the other cheek." At least two of them had sobriquets which suggest that they were linked with militant activists. One was Simon, called "The Zealot," and the other was Judas, called "Iscariot." There is an uncanny resemblance between Iscariot and *sicarii*, the word used by Josephus to identify the knife-wielding, homicidal dagger men. And in certain Old Latin manuscripts Judas is actually called *Zelotes*.

Two other disciples had warlike nicknames—James and John, the sons of Zebedee. They were called "Boanerges," which Mark translates from Aramaic as "Sons of Thunder" and which could also mean "the fierce, wrathful ones." The sons of Zebedee deserved their reputation. At one point in the gospel narrative they want to destroy an entire Samaritan village because the people had not welcomed Jesus.

The gospels also indicate that some of the disciples carried swords and were prepared to resist arrest. Just before being taken into custody, Jesus said, "He that hath no sword, let him sell his garment and buy one." This prompted the disciples to show him two swords—indicating that at least two of them were not only habitually armed but had kept their swords concealed under their clothes . . . like dagger men.

All four gospels record the fact that the disciples put up armed resistance at the moment of Jesus' capture. After the Passover supper, Jesus and his inner circle slipped away to a garden in Gethsemane where they prepared to spend the night. Guided by Judas Iscariot, the High Priest and his men burst in on them as Jesus was praying and the rest were sleeping. The disciples drew their swords and a brief struggle ensued, during which one of the temple policemen lost an ear. As soon as the police grabbed Jesus, the disciples stopped fighting and ran away into the night. According to Matthew, Jesus told one of his disciples to sheath his sword, a command which the disciple obeyed but was obviously unprepared to hear, since he immediately deserted.

In the gospel narrative, the price given to Judas resembles Herodias' denunciation of John the Baptist. If Judas was in fact *Zelotes*—a zealot-bandit—he might have betrayed Jesus for any number of tactical or strategic reasons, but never simply for money. (One theory is that Jesus wasn't being militant enough.) By identifying Judas' motivation as pure greed, the gospels may simply have repeated the kind of distortion that Josephus and the Romans automatically employed with respect to all zealot-bandits. But zealot-bandits were prepared to kill without getting paid—that at least should be clear from the events described in the previous chapter.

Why did the disciples all run away, and why did Simon Peter deny Jesus three times before the night was over? Because as Jews they shared with Caiaphas the lifestyle consciousness of their ancestors and understood that the messiah was to be an invincible, wonder-working military prince.

All this leads to one conclusion: The lifestyle consciousness shared by Jesus and his inner circle of disciples was not the lifestyle consciousness of a peaceful messiah. Although the gospels clearly intend to deny Jesus the capacity to carry out violent political acts, they preserve what seems to be an undercurrent of contradictory events and sayings which link John the Baptist and Jesus to the military-messianic tradition and implicate them in the guerrilla warfare. The reason for this is that by the time the first gospel was written, nonpeaceful events and sayings which had been attributed to Jesus by eyewitnesses and by unimpeachable apostolic sources were widely known among the faithful. The writers of the gospels shifted the balance of the Jesus cult's lifestyle consciousness in the direction of a peaceful messiah, but they could not entirely expunge the traces of continuity with the military-messianic tradition. The ambiguity of the gospels in this regard is best demonstrated by arranging some of Jesus' most peaceful statements in one column and the unexpected negations in another:

Blessed are the peacemakers. (Matthew 5:9)	Think not that I am come to send peace on earth, I come not to send peace but a sword. (Matthew 10:34)
Whosoever shall smite thee on thy right cheek, turn to him the other also. (Matthew 5:39)	Suppose ye that I come to give peace on earth? I will tell you nay, but rather division. (Luke 12:51)
All that take the sword shall perish with the sword. (Matthew 26:52)	He that hath no sword, let him sell his garments and buy one. (Luke 22:36)
Love thine enemies; do good to them that hate you. (Luke 6:27)	And when he had made a scourge of small cords, he drove them out of the temple ... and poured out the changer's money and overthrew the tables. (John 2:15)

I should also note at this point the obviously false construction traditionally given to what Jesus said when he was asked if Jews ought to pay taxes to the Romans: "Render unto Caesar that which is Caesar's and unto God that which is God's." This could mean only one thing to the Galileans who had participated in Judas of Galilee's tax revolt—namely, "Don't pay." For Judas of Galilee had said that everything in Palestine belonged to God. But the authors of the Gospels and their readers probably knew nothing about

Judas of Galilee, so they preserved Jesus' highly provocative response on the mistaken assumption that it showed a genuinely conciliatory attitude toward the Roman government.

After they had captured him, the Romans and their Jewish clients continued to treat Jesus as if he were the leader of an actual or intended military-messianic uprising. The Jewish high court put him on trial for having made blasphemous and false prophecies. He was quickly found guilty and turned over to Pontius Pilate for a second trial on secular charges. The reason for this seems clear. As I showed in the chapter on cargo, popular messiahs in colonial contexts are always guilty of a politico-religious crime, never merely a religious one. The Romans had no interest in Jesus' violation of the natives' religious codes, but they were vitally concerned with his threat to destroy the colonial government.

Caiaphas' predictions about how the crowd would react once Jesus was shown to be helpless was soon fully vindicated. Pilate publicly exhibited the condemned man and not a voice was lifted in protest. Pilate even went so far as to offer to free Jesus, if the mob wanted him back. The gospels claim that Pilate made this offer because he himself believed that Jesus was innocent. But Pilate, you will recall, was a tricky, heavy-fisted military hard-liner who kept having trouble with the Jerusalem mob. According to Josephus, Pilate once lured several thousand people into the Jerusalem stadium, surrounded them with soldiers, and threatened to cut their heads off. On another occasion his men infiltrated the mob by wearing civilian clothes over their armor and on a given signal clubbed everybody in sight. In presenting Jesus to the rabble that had only yesterday adored and protected him, Pilate was making use of the inexorable logic of the military-messianic tradition to impress the natives with their own stupidity. There stood their supposedly divine liberator, King of the Holy Jewish Empire, utterly helpless against a few Roman soldiers. The crowd may very well have responded by demanding that Jesus be killed as a religious imposter, but Pilate was not interested in crucifying religious charlatans. To the Romans, Jesus was just another subversive who deserved the same fate as all the other rabble-rousing bandits and revolutionaries who kept crawling out of the desert. That was why the title on Jesus' cross read "King of the Jews."

S. G. F. Brandon, a former dean of the School of Theology of the University of Manchester, reminds us that Jesus was not crucified alone; the gospels report that his fate was shared by two other convicted criminals. What was the crime for which Jesus' companions were put to death? In English language versions of the gospels, the two are said to be "thieves." But the original Greek manuscript term for them was *lestai,* precisely the same term that Josephus used when he wanted to refer to the zealot-bandits. Brandon believes that we can be even more specific about who these "bandits" actually were. Mark states that at the time of Jesus' trial, the Jerusalem jail contained a number of prisoners "that had made insurrection." If Jesus' companions were drawn from these insurrectionists, the grisly scene at Golgotha obtains a unity otherwise lacking: the supposed messianic King of the Jews at the center, flanked by two zealot-bandits—a scene compatible with everything that we know about the mentality of colonial officers intent on teaching law and order to rebellious natives.

All four gospels converge on the somber spectacle of Jesus

suffering on the cross with the disciples nowhere in sight. The disciples could not believe that a messiah would permit himself to be crucified. They did not as yet have the slightest inkling that the Jesus cult was to be the cult of a peaceful rather than a vengeful savior. In fact, as Brandon points out, the gospel of Mark gains its dramatic thrust from the failure of the disciples to grasp the reason why their messsiah will not destroy his enemies and will not save himself from being killed.

It was only after the disappearance of Jesus' body from the tomb that his apparent lack of messianic power came to be understood. A number of disciples began to have visions, which made them realize that the usual test of messiahship—victory—did not apply to Jesus. Inspired by their visions, they took the important but not entirely unprecedented step of arguing that Jesus' death didn't prove he was another false messiah; rather, it proved that God had provided the Jews with another climactic opportunity to show themselves worthy of the covenant. Jesus would return if people repented for doubting him and asked God's forgiveness.

There is no reason to suppose that this reinterpretation of the significance of Jesus' death led at once to a rejection of the military and political import of his messiahship. Much evidence supports the view argued persuasively by Professor Brandon, that most of the Jews who awaited Jesus' return in the period between his crucifixion and the fall of Jerusalem continued to expect a messiah who would overthrow Rome and make Jerusaem the capital of the Holy Jewish Empire. At the outset of the Acts of the Apostles, which is Luke's account of what happened after Jesus was killed, the political significance of Jesus' return is uppermost in the minds of the apostles. The first question they put to the risen Jesus is: "Lord, wilt thou at this time restore again the kingdom to Israel?" Another New Testament source, the Book of Revelations, depicts the returning Jesus as a many-crowned rider on a white horse who judges and makes war, who has eyes as "a flame of fire," wears a garment "dipped in blood," and rules the nations with "a rod of iron," and who returns to "tread the winepress of the fury of the wrath of God Almighty."

There is also some convergent evidence on this point from the Dead Sea Scrolls. I said a moment ago that the idea of messiah returning from the dead was not unprecedented. The Dead Sea Scrolls refer to a "teacher of righteousness" who is killed by his enemies but returns to fulfill the messianic task. Like the Quamranites, the first Jewish Christians organized themselves into a commune while awaiting the return of their "teacher of righteousness."

The Acts of the Apostles states:

All that believed were together and had all things in common, and sold their possessions and goods, and parted them among all, according as any man had need. . . . Neither was there any among them that lacked, for as many as were possessors of lands or houses sold them, and brought the prices of the things sold and laid them down at the apostles' feet.

It is of considerable interest that the Dead Sea Scrolls contain prescriptions for establishing communities of penitent Jews in the cities to be organized along the same communistic lines. This is additional evidence that the Quamran militants and the Jewish Christians were either responding in similar ways to similar conditions or were actually aspects or branches of one and the same military-messianic movement.

As I indicated at the beginning of this chapter, the image of Jesus as the peaceful messiah was probably not perfected until after the fall of Jerusalem. During the interval between Jesus' death and the writing of the first gospel, the groundwork for a cult of peaceful messianism was laid by Paul. But those for whom Jesus was primarily a Jewish military-messianic redeemer dominated the movement throughout the period of expanding guerrilla activity leading up to the confrontation of 68 A.D. The practical setting in which the gospels were written—gospels which depict a purely peaceful and universal messiah—was the aftermath of the unsuccessful Jewish war against Rome. A purely peaceful messiah became a practical necessity when the generals who had just defeated the Jewish messianic revolutionaries—Vespasian and Titus—became the rulers of the Roman Empire. Before that defeat, it had been a practical necessity for the Jewish Christians in Jerusalem to remain loyal to Judaism. After that defeat, the Jewish Christians in Jerusalem could no longer dominate the Christian communities in other parts of the empire, least of all those Christians who lived in Rome at the sufferance of Vespasian and Titus. In the aftermath of the unsuccessful messianic war, it quickly became a practical necessity for Christians to deny that their cult had arisen out of the Jewish belief in a messiah who was going to topple the Roman Empire.

The Jerusalem commune was led by a triumvirate called "the pillars" in the Acts of the Apostles, consisting of James, Peter, and John. Among these, James, identified by Paul as "the Lord's Brother" (precise genealogical connection unknown), soon emerged as the preeminent figure. It was James who led the struggle against Paul's attempt to obscure the Jewish military-messianic origins of the Jesus movement.

Although Jerusalem remained the center of Christianity until 70 A.D., the new cult soon spread beyond Palestine to many of the communities of Jewish merchants, artisans, and scholars found in every major city and town of the Roman Empire. The overseas Jews learned about Jesus from missionaries who toured the foreign synagogues. Paul, the most important of these missionaries, was born Saul of Tarsus, a Greek-speaking Jew whose father had acquired Roman citizenship for himself and his family. Paul insisted that he had become an apostle of Jesus by the authority of revelation and without any direct contact with the original apostles in Jerusalem. In his letter to the Galatians, written sometime between 49 and 57 A.D., Paul said that he had been missionizing Arabia and Damascus for three years and had never talked to any of the original apostles. The letter states that at that time he visited briefly with Simon Peter and talked with James, "the Lord's Brother."

For the next fifteen years Paul was on the road again, traveling from city to city. His first converts were almost invariably Jews. This had to be the case because it was the Jews who were most familiar with the prophetic lineage that Paul claimed Jesus fulfilled. Even if Paul had not studied with rabbis, had not spoken Hebrew, and had not considered himself a Jew, he would still have found the Jews scattered throughout the eastern portion of the Roman Empire the people most likely to respond to the appeal of the Jesus cult. Not only were the Jews one of the largest groups of displaced persons in the empire, but they were among the most influential and up to 71 A.D. enjoyed many privileges which were denied to other ethnics. Paul had between three and six million Jews to proselytize outside of Palestine—more than twice as many as James had to proselytize within Palestine—and virtually every one of the foreign Jews lived in a city or town.

Paul made a special effort to recruit among non-Jews whenever he was rebuffed by an overseas Jewish community. But this in itself was no novelty. Attracted by the social and economic advantages which Jews enjoyed as a result of their long experience in cosmopolitan settings, there always had been a steady stream of converts to Judaism. Male converts were welcome as Jews as long as they were willing to obey the commandments and be circumcised. The greatest novelty associated with Paul's proselytizing was not his messianic message, but his willingness to baptize non-Jews as Jewish Christians without bothering to have them circumcised or certified as Jews.

The Acts of the Apostles states that Paul returned to Jerusalem after a prolonged absence, and pleaded with James and the Jerusalem elders not to interfere with his efforts at converting non-Jews to Christianity. James's verdict was that non-Jews could become Christians without submitting to circumcision provided they renounced idolatry, fornication, and meat that was strangled or bloody. But James and the Jerusalem communards insisted that uncircumcised Christians were inferior to Jewish Christians. Paul reports that when Simon Peter visited him in Antioch, all the Christians ate together. But with the arrival of a commission of inquiry sent out by James, Simon Peter immediately stopped eating with the uncircumcised Christians, "fearing them that were of the Circumcision"—that is, fearing that the Jewish Christian commissioners would tell James.

It was to Paul's advantage, given his overseas constituency, to underplay the privileged role to be allocated to the children of Israel in the Holy Jewish Empire. It was also to his advantage to ignore the worldly military and political components in Jesus' messianic mission. But Paul's ecumenical innovations created a strategic problem that he was never able to solve. Inevitably it brought him into deeper conflict with James and the Jerusalem communards, since the survival of the Jerusalem Christians depended on their ability to maintain their standing as bona-fide Jewish patriots. In order to survive amid the various factions involved in the escalating war with Rome, it was essential that James continue to worship in the Jerusalem temple and that his followers maintain an image of devotion to Jewish law. Their faith in Jahweh's covenant had been increased, not diminished, by their belief that Jesus would soon reappear.

Paul was accused of urging Jews in foreign cities to disregard the laws of Judaism and of treating Jew and non-Jew as if there were no difference between them—as if Jew and gentile were equally entitled to the blessings of the forthcoming messianic redemption. If such an interpretation of the Jesus cult were ever to spread to Jerusalem, James and his followers were doomed. In Brandon's words: "From the Jewish point of view, such a presentation was not only theologically outrageous, it amounted to apostasy of the most shocking kind, involving both race and religion."

The preserved evidence of Jesus' reported actions and sayings provides no support for Paul's attempt to scrap the distinction between Jew and non-Jew in the overseas communes. In the Gospel according to Mark, for example, a

Syrian Greek woman falls at Jesus' feet and begs him to drive out the devils from her daughter. Jesus refuses: "Let the children first be filled: for it is not meet to take the children's bread and to cast it to the dogs." The Syrian Greek woman argues back, saying: "The dogs under the table eat the childrens' crumbs," whereupon Jesus relents and cures the woman's daughter. "Children" here can only mean "children of Israel" and "dogs" can only mean non-Jews, especially enemies like the Syrian Greeks. Incidents and sayings of this sort were preserved in Mark and the other gospels for the same reason that the other vengeful and ethnocentric sayings and actions could not be entirely expunged. There were lively oral traditions upon which the gospels were based. Too many eyewitnesses like James, Peter, and John were still active, eyewitnesses who insisted on the authenticity of the military-messianic and ethnocentric themes. Besides, Mark was Jewish by birth and therefore was probably never entirely free from some degree of ambivalence about the ethnic distinctions that had formerly been insisted upon by the founders of the Jerusalem mother "church."

To protect the Jerusalem commune, James dispatched rival missionaries instructed to preserve the Judaic significance of Christianity; they were not above jeopardizing Paul's following by impugning his credentials. Paul was vulnerable to these attacks because he admitted that he had never seen Jesus except in a vision. Moreover, he continued to need the support of the foreign synagogues. So, in 59 A.D., despite forebodings and oracular warnings, Paul decided to return to Jerusalem and have it out with his accusers.

Paul appeared before James as an accused person appears

before a judge. James admonished Paul by noting that there were thousands of Jews in Jerusalem who believed in Jesus, yet they were all "zealous of the law." He then ordered Paul to demonstrate that he was a loyal Jew and that the charges against him were unfounded—to demonstrate "that thou walkest orderly and keepest the law." He demanded that Paul submit to seven days of purificatory rites in the Jerusalem temple. Paul accepted these demands, proving: (1) James, the Lord's Brother, was the supreme leader of Christendom at that time; (2) James and the Jewish Christians still worshiped in the temple—they had no separate "church"; (3) the Jewish Christians believed that Jesus would return to fulfill the Davidic covenant by making Jerusalem the center of the Holy Jewish Empire; (4) all baptized penitent believers in Jesus and Jahweh would be redeemed, but Jewish Christians would be redeemed more than the rest.

Paul's attempt to reaffirm his loyalty to the Jewish national ideal was cut short, undoubtedly by treachery. A group of pilgrims from Asia recognized him, stirred up a mob, dragged him from the temple, and started to beat him to death. Only the timely intervention of the Roman captain of the guard saved Paul on that occasion. Brought to trial by the high priests, he again narrowly escaped death. More plots were laid against him, but he finally managed to escape from Palestine by invoking his Roman citizenship and demanding that he be tried by Romans, not by Jews. He was sent to Rome and kept under house arrest, but what happened to him afterwards is not definitely known. What probably happened to him is that he was martyred in 64 A.D., when the Emperor Nero decided to blame a huge fire in Rome—which his enemies said he himself had set to clear out the slums near his palace—on a convenient new bloodthirsty sect that had arisen among the Jews, members of which were "enemies of mankind."

Too late for Paul, the outbreak of full-scale war in Palestine drastically altered the political context of his aborted mission. By 70 A.D. the Jewish Christian mother "church" in Jerusalem no longer held the upper hand over the overseas Christian communities. It ceased to be a significant force, if it can be said in any sense to have survived the fall of Jerusalem. The protracted revolution of 68–73 thoroughly embittered relationships between the overseas Jews and the Romans. Also, it catapulted the very persons responsible for the defeat of the Jews into control of the empire. In 71 A.D. Vespasian and his son Titus held a stupendous triumphal procession—commemorated on the Arch of Titus in Rome—during which Jewish prisoners and spoils were marched through the streets while the last zealot-bandit commander of Jerusalem, Simon ben Gioras, was strangled in the Forum. Vespasian thereafter dealt harshly with the Jews in the empire, restricting their liberties and diverting their temple tax to the treasury of Saturn. During the remainder of the first century A.D., anti-Semitism became an established feature of Roman life and letters; it was met with smoldering defiance, insurrection, and intensified repressions that led to the second Armageddon of Bar Kochva in 135 A.D.

From the stress placed by Mark upon the destruction of the temple in Jerusalem as a punishment for the killers of Jesus, Brandon infers that this gospel—the first to be composed and the model for the others—was written in Rome after the fall of Jerusalem. As Brandon says, it was probably written in direct response to the great victory celebration of 71 A.D.

The appropriate conditions for the spread of the cult of a peaceful messiah were at last present in full force. Jewish Christians now readily joined with gentile converts to convince the Romans that *their* messiah was different from the zealot-bandit messiahs who had caused the war and who were continuing to make trouble: Christians, unlike Jews, were harmless pacifists with no secular ambitions. The Christian Kingdom of God was not of this world; Christian salvation lay in eternal life beyond the grave; the Christian messiah had died to bring eternal life to all mankind; his teaching posed no threat to the Romans, only to the Jews; the Romans were absolved of any guilt in Jesus' death; the Jews alone had killed him while Pontius Pilate stood by, helplessly unable to prevent it.

The secret of the peaceful messiah lay on the battlefields and in the aftermath of two earthly Armageddons. The cult of the peaceful messiah as we know it would not have prospered had the course of battle gone against the "Sons of Darkness."

The primary source of converts to this new religion—if not in number, certainly in influence—continued to be urban Jews scattered all over the eastern Mediterranean. Contrary to legend, Christianity made no headway at all among the great mass of peasants and slaves who constituted the bulk of the population of the empire. As the historian Salo W. Baron points out, *paganus*, the Latin word for "peasant," became for the Christians a synonym for "heathen." Christianity was eminently the religion of the displaced ethnic urbanites. "In cities where Jews had often amounted to one third of the population and more, this, so to speak, new variety of Judaism marched triumphantly ahead."

Jews who remained Jews were far more the victims of Roman persecution than Jews who became Christians. The age of full-scale imperial persecution of Christians did not begin with Nero, but much later—after 150 A.D. By that time, because they were concentrated in the urban centers, had infiltrated the Roman upper class, maintained effective social welfare programs, and were building a fiscally independent, international corporation led by skilled administrators, the Christian churches had once again become a political threat to Roman law and order. They had become a "state within a state."

I shall have to refrain from following out the chain of worldly events that eventually led to the establishment of Christianity as the religion of the Roman Empire. But this much should be said: When the Emperor Constantine took that momentous initiative, Christianity was no longer the cult of the peaceful messiah. Constantine's conversion took place in 311 A.D. as he led a small army across the Alps. Wearily approaching Rome he saw a vision of the cross standing above the sun, and on the cross he saw the words IN HOC SIGNO VINCES—"By this sign you will conquer." Jesus appeared to Constantine and directed him to emblazon his military standard with the cross. Under this strange new banner, Constantine's soldiers went on to win a decisive victory. They regained the empire and thereby guaranteed that the cross of the peaceful messiah would preside over the deaths of untold millions of Christian soldiers and their enemies down to the present day.

Broomsticks and Sabbats

JUST AS big men helped us to understand the practical significance of messiahs, now that we know something about messiahs we will be better able to understand the practical significance of witches. But once again I must warn you that the relationship won't be obvious. A number of preliminary matters must be considered before the connection can be drawn.

It is estimated that five hundred thousand people were convicted of witchcraft and burned to death in Europe between the fifteenth and seventeenth centuries. Their crimes: a pact with the Devil; journeys through the air over vast distances mounted on broomsticks; unlawful assembly at sabbats; worship of the Devil; kissing the Devil under the tail; copulation with incubi, male devils equipped with ice-cold penises; copulation with succubi, female devils.

Other more mundane charges were often added: killing the neighbor's cow; causing hailstorms; ruining the crops; stealing and eating babies. But many a witch was executed for no crime other than flying through the air to attend a sabbat.

I want to distinguish two separate witchcraft riddles. First there is the problem of why anyone should believe that witches fly through the air on broomsticks. And then there is the largely separate problem of why such a notion should have become so popular during the sixteenth and seventeenth centuries. I think practical and mundane solutions can be found for both of these puzzles. To begin, let's concentrate on the explanation of why and how witches flew to sabbats.

Despite the existence of a large number of "confessions," little is actually known about the case histories of self-acknowledged witches. Some historians have maintained that the whole bizarre complex—the Devil's pact, the broomstick flight, and the sabbat—was the invention of the witch burners rather than of the burnt witches. But as we shall see, at least some of the accused had a pretrial sense of being witches and fervently believed that they could fly through the air and have intercourse with devils.

The trouble with the "confessions" is that they were usually obtained while the accused witch was being tortured. Torture was routinely applied until the witch confessed to having made a pact with the Devil and having flown to a sabbat. It was continued until the witch named the other people who were present at the sabbat. If a witch attempted to retract a confession, torture was applied even more intensely until the original confession was reconfirmed. This left a person accused of witchcraft with the choice between dying once and for all at the stake or being returned repeatedly to the torture chambers. Most people opted for the stake. As a reward for their cooperative attitude, penitent witches could look forward to being strangled before the fire was lit.

Let me describe a typical case among the hundreds documented by the historian of European witchcraft, Charles Henry Lea. It took place in 1601 in Offenburg, a city located in what later became West Germany. Under torture, two vagrant women had confessed to being witches. When urged to identify the other people whom they had seen at the sabbat, they named the baker's wife, Else Gwinner. Else Gwinner was brought before the examiners on October 31, 1601, and stoutly denied any knowledge of witchery. She was urged to spare herself unnecessary suffering, but she persisted in her denial. Her hands were tied behind her back and she was hoisted off the ground by a rope tied to her wrists—a system known as the strappado. She began to scream, said that she would confess, and begged to be let down. When she was let down, all that she would say was "Father forgive them, for they know not what they do." Torture was reapplied but only succeeded in rendering her unconscious. She was removed to prison and was tortured again on November 7 by being hoisted three times on the strappado—with progressively heavier weights attached to her body. On the third hoist she shrieked that she could not endure it. They let her down, and she confessed that she had enjoyed "the love of a demon." The examiners were dissatisfied and wanted to know more. They hoisted her again with the heaviest weights, exhorting her to tell the truth. When she was set down again, Else insisted that "her confessions were lies to escape the suffering" and that the "truth was that she was innocent." Meanwhile the examiners had arrested

Else's daughter Agathe. They took Agathe to a cell and beat her until she confessed that both she and her mother were witches and that they had caused crop failures in order to raise the price of bread. When Else and Agathe were brought together, the daughter retracted the part that implicated her mother. But as soon as Agathe was alone with the examiners, she reconfirmed the confession and begged not to be brought face-to-face with her mother again.

Else was taken to another prison and worked on with thumbscrews. At each pause she reconfirmed her innocence. Finally she again admitted that she had a demon lover but nothing more. Torture was resumed on December 11 after she once again denied all guilt. On this occasion, she passed out. Cold water was dashed in her face, and she screamed and begged to be let go. "But as soon as the torture was intermittent she revoked her confession." At last she confessed that her demon lover had taken her on two flights to the sabbat. The examiners demanded to know whom she had seen at these sabbats. Else named two people—Frau Spiess and Frau Weyss. She promised to reveal more names later. But on December 13, she revoked her confession, despite the efforts of a priest who confronted her with additional evidence obtained from Agathe. On December 15 the examiners told her that they were going "to continue the torture without mercy or compassion until she should tell the truth." She became faint, but asserted her innocence. She repeated her previous confession but insisted that she was mistaken about having seen Frau Spiess and Frau Weyss at the sabbat: "There was such a crowd and confusion that identification was difficult, especially as all present covered their faces as much as possible." Despite the threat of additional torture, she refused to seal her confession with a final oath. Else Gwinner was burned to death on December 21, 1601.

In addition to the strappado, the rack, and thumbscrew, the witch hunters used chairs with sharp points, heated from below, shoes with pricks, bands with needles, red-hot irons, red-hot pincers, starvation, and sleeplessness. One contemporary critic of the witch craze, Johann Matthäus Meyfarth, wrote that he would give a fortune if he could banish the memory of what he had seen take place in the torture chambers:

I have seen the limbs forced asunder, the eyes driven out of the head, the feet torn from the legs, the sinews twisted from the joints, the shoulder blades wrung from their place, the deep veins swollen, the superficial veins driven in, the victim hoisted aloft and now dropped, now revolved around, head undermost and feet uppermost. I have seen the executioner flog with the scourge, and smite with rods, and crush with screws and load down with weights, and stick with needles, and bind around with cords, and burn with brimstone, and baste with oil and singe with torches. In short, I can bear witness, I can describe, I can deplore how the human body is violated.

Throughout the witchcraft craze, any confession made under torture had to be confirmed before sentence was passed. So the records of the witchcraft cases always contain the formula: "So and so has of free will confirmed the confession made under torture." But as Meyfarth indicates, such confessions were worthless for the purpose of separating genuine from spurious witches. What does it mean, he asks, when one encounters the formula: "Margaretha, before the bench of justice, has of free will confirmed the confession made under torture"?

It means that, when after unendurable torment she confessed, the executioner said to her, "If you intend to deny what you have confessed, tell me now and I will do better. If you deny before the court, you come back to my hands and you will find that I have only played with you thus far, for I will treat you so that it would draw tears from a stone." When Margaretha is brought before the court, she is in fetters and her hands so tied "that it brings the blood." By her side stand the gaoler and executioner and behind her armed guards. After the reading of the confession, the executioner asks her whether she confirms it or not.

The historian Hugh Trevor-Roper insists that many confessions were made to public authorities without any evidence of torture. But even such "spontaneous" and "freely given" admissions must be evaluated against the more subtle forms of terror that the examiners and judges had at their disposal. It was established practice among the witchcraft examiners first to threaten torture, then to describe the instruments to be used, and then to display the actual instruments. Confessions might be elicted anywhere along the way. The effects of these threats probably shaded off onto pretrial "confessions" that today seem to be "spontaneous." I don't deny the existence of genuine confessions or of "genuine" witches, but it seems to me highly perverse on the part of modern specialists to treat the use of torture as if it were a minor aspect of the witchcraft inquiries. Examiners were never satisfied until the confessed witches named additional suspects, who subsequently were routinely indicted and tortured themselves.

Meyfarth mentions a case in which an old woman who had been tortured for three days admitted to the man whom she had named, "I have never seen you at the sabbat, but to end the torture I had to accuse someone. You came into my mind because, as I was being led to prison, you met me and said you would never have believed it of me. I beg forgiveness, but if I were tortured again, I would accuse you again." The woman was returned to the rack and confirmed her original story. Without torture, I cannot see how the witchcraft craze could have claimed so many victims, no matter how many people really believed that they flew to the sabbat.

Virtually every society in the world has some sort of witchcraft concept. But the European witch craze was more ferocious, lasted longer, and produced more victims than any other similar outbreak. When witchcraft is suspected in primitive societies, painful ordeals may be used as part of the attempt to determine guilt or innocence. But in no cases that I know of are witches tortured into confessing the identity of other witches.

Even in Europe, it was only after 1480 that torture was used this way. Before 1000 A.D. no one was executed if a neighbor allegedly saw them with the Devil. People accused each other of being sorcerers or witches and of having supernatural powers to do evil. And there was much speculation about certain women who could journey through the air and cover great distances at enormous speeds. But the authorities took little interest in systematically hunting down witches and forcing them to confess their crimes. In fact, the Catholic Church originally insisted that there were no such things as witches flying through the air. In the year 1000 A.D. it was forbidden to believe that such flights really took place;

later, after 1480, it was forbidden to believe that they did not take place. In 1000 A.D. the Church officially maintained that the ride of the witches was an illusion produced by the Devil. Five hundred years later, the Church officially maintained that those who claimed that the ride was merely an illusion were themselves in league with the Devil.

The older viewpoint was governed by a document called the Canon Episcopi. Referring to the people who believed that bands of witches fly through the night, the Canon warned: "The faithless mind thinks these things happen not in the spirit but in the body." In other words, the Devil can get you to believe that you or others go on night rides, but neither you nor they can *really* do it. The test of what "really" means and of its decisive difference from later definitions of "reality" is that no one whom you or your fellow dreamers believe was along on the ride can be charged with wrongdoing. It is only a dream that they were there, and others are not to be held accountable for what they do in your dreams. The dreamer, however, is having evil thoughts and should be punished—not by being burned but by being excommunicated.

It took several centuries to reverse the Canon Episcopi, making it an heretical offense to deny that witches transported themselves in body as well as in spirit. Once the reality of the journey had been established, it became possible to question each confessed witch concerning the other people who were at the sabbat. Torture applied at this juncture guaranteed that a breeder reaction would take place. As in advanced model atomic furnaces, every burnt witch automatically led to two or more additional candidates for burning. To help the system run smoothly, there were additional refinements. Expenses were kept down by forcing the witch's family to pay the bill for the services of the torturers and the executioners. The family was also billed for the cost of the fagots and for the banquet which the judges held after the burning. Considerable enthusiasm for witch-hunting could be built up among local officials, since they were empowered to confiscate the entire estate of any person condemned for witchcraft.

Aspects of the mature witch-hunt system were perfected as early as the thirteenth century, but not as part of the struggle against witches. The Church first authorized the use of torture not against witches, but against members of illicit ecclesiastical organizations that were springing up all over Europe and threatening to break the monopoly that Rome held on tithes and sacraments. By the thirteenth century, for example, the Albigensians (also called Cathari) in southern France had developed into a powerful independent ecclesiastical body with its own clergy who met openly under the protection of dissident factions of the French nobility. The Pope had to call for a holy war—the Albigensian Crusade—to preserve southern France for Christendom. The Albigensians were eventually exterminated, but many other heretical sects such as the Waldenses and the Vaudois took their place. To combat these subversive movements, the Church gradually created the Inquisition, a special paramilitary office whose sole function was to extirpate heresy. Pursued by the Inquisition in France, Italy, and Germany, the heretics went underground, formed clandestine cells, and held secret meetings. Finding their efforts thwarted by the enemy's secret operations, the papal inquisitors requested authorization to use torture to force heretics to confess and name their accomplices. This authorization was granted in the middle of the thirteenth century by Pope Alexander IV.

While the Waldensians and Vaudois were being tortured, witches still enjoyed the protection of the Canon Episcopi. Witchcraft was a crime, but it was not heresy—since the sabbat was a figment of the imagination. But with the passage of time, papal inquisitors became more and more disturbed by the lack of jurisdiction over witchcraft cases. Witchcraft, they argued, was no longer what it used to be in the days of the Canon Episcopi. A new and much more dangerous kind of witch had developed—a witch that actually could fly to sabbats. And these sabbats were just like the secret meetings of the other heretical sects, only the rites were even more loathsome. If witches could be tortured like other heretics, their confessions would lead to the discovery of a vast body of secret conspirators. At last Rome yielded. A Pope named Innocent issued a bull in 1484 that authorized inquisitors Heinrich Institor and Jakob Sprenger to use the full power of the Inquisition to extirpate witches throughout Germany.

Institor and Sprenger convinced the Pope with arguments which were subsequently presented in their book *The Hammer of the Witches*, forever after the compleat witch hunter's manual. It is true, they admitted, that some witches only imagine that they attend the sabbat; but many are actually transported there bodily. In either event, it is the same thing, since the witch who goes only in imagination sees what is taking place as reliably as the one whose body is transported. As for those cases where a husband has sworn that his wife was in bed at his side while others have testified that she was at a sabbat, it was not his wife whom he touched, but a devil taking her place. Perhaps the Canon Episcopi had claimed that the flight was only imaginary, but there was nothing imaginary at all about the damage the witches were doing. "Who is so dense as to maintain . . . that all their witchcraft and injuries are phantastic and imaginary, when the contrary is evident to the senses of everybody?" Every conceivable misfortune—loss of cattle and crops, death of children, illness, aches and pains, infidelity, sterility and insanity—has been caused by witchcraft. *The Hammer of the Witches* concluded with a detailed account of how witches were to be identified, arraigned, tried, tortured, convicted, and sentenced. The witch-hunting system was now complete, ready to be applied throughout Europe for the next two hundred years, with devastating results, by both Catholic and Protestant witch hunters. Ready to produce, year in and year out, an unending supply of new witches to replace the ones who were imprisoned or burned.

Why was the Canon Episcopi overruled? The simplest explanation is that the inquisitors were right: Witches were meeting at secret sabbats—even if they didn't get there on their broomsticks—and they actually constituted as much of a threat to the security of Christendom as the Waldenses or the other clandestine religious movements.

Recent discoveries about the practical basis of broomstick flight have made this theory untenable. Professor Michael Harner of the New School for Social Research has shown that European witches were popularly associated with the use of magical salves and ointments. Before riding through the air on their broomsticks, the witches "anointed" themselves. One of the typical cases cited by Harner is that of a witch in seventeenth-century England who confessed that "before they are carried to their meetings, they anoint their Foreheads and their Hand-wrists with an Oyl the Spirit brings them (which smells raw)." Other English witches reported that the "Oyl" had a greenish color and that it was applied to the forehead with a feather. In early accounts, the witch is said to have applied the ointment to a staff, after which "she ambled and galloped through thick and thin, when and in what manner she listed." Anointing of both the pole and the body is reported in a fifteenth-century source also cited by Harner: "They anoint a staff and ride on it . . . or anoint themselves under the arms and in other hairy places." Another source states: "Witches, male and female, who have pact with the devil, anointing themselves with certain unguents and reciting certain words are carried by night to distant lands."

Andrés Laguna, a sixteenth-century physician practicing in Lorraine, described the discovery of a witch's jar "half filled with a certain green unguent . . . with which they were anointing themselves: whose odor was so heavy and offensive that it showed that it was composed of herbs cold and soporiferous to the ultimate degree, which are hemlock, nightshade, henbane and mandrake." Laguna obtained a canister full of this ointment and used it to carry out an experiment on the wife of a hangman in Metz. He anointed this woman from head to toe, whereupon "she suddenly slept such a sound sleep, with her eyes open like a rabbit (she also fittingly looked like a boiled hare), that I could not imagine how to wake her." When Laguna finally managed to get her up, she had been sleeping for thirty-six hours. She complained: "Why do you wake me at such an inopportune time?

I was surrounded by all the pleasures and delights of the world." Then she smiled at her husband who was standing there, "all stinking of hanged men," and said to him, "Knavish one, know that I have made you a cuckold, and with a lover younger and better than you."

Harner has brought together a number of such reported experiments with ointments involving the witches themselves All the subjects fell into a deep sleep, and upon being awakened, insisted that they had been away on a long journey. So the secret of the ointment was known by many people who lived at the time of the witch craze, even though modern historians have generally tended to forget or minimize it. The best eyewitness statement on the subject was made by one of Galileo's colleagues, Giambattista della Porta, who obtained the formula for an ointment containing nightshade.

As soon as it is finished, they anoint the part of the body, having rubbed themselves very thoroughly before, so they grow rosy. ... Thus on some moonlit night they think they are carried off to banquets, music, dances, and coupling with young men, which they desire most of all. So great is the force of imagination and the appearance of the images, that the part of the brain called memory is almost full of this sort of thing; and since they themselves, by inclination of nature, are extremely prone to belief, they take hold of the images in such a way that the mind itself is changed and thinks of nothing else day or night.

Harner, who has been studying the use of hallucinogens by shamans among the Jívaro Indians of Peru, thinks that the active hallucinogenic agent in the witch ointments was atropine, a powerful alkaloid found in such European plants as mandrake, henbane, and belladonna (beautiful lady!) or deadly nightshade. The outstanding feature of atropine is that it is absorbable through the intact skin, a feature used to advantage in belladonna skin plasters for the relief of muscular pains. Several modern experimenters have re-created witches' ointments based on formulas preserved in old documents. One group in Göttingen, Germany, reports falling into a twenty-four-hour sleep during which they dreamed of "wild rides, frenzied dancing, and other weird adventures of the type connected with medieval orgies." Another experimenter who merely inhaled the fumes of henbane speaks of the "crazy sensation that my feet were growing lighter, expanding and breaking loose from my body ... at the same time I experienced an intoxicating sensation of flying."

Why the staff or broom that can still be seen between the legs of modern-day Halloween witches? According to Harner, it was no mere phallic symbol:

The use of the staff or broom was undoubtedly more than a symbolic Freudian act, serving as an applicator for the atropine-containing plant to the sensitive vaginal membranes, as well as providing the suggestion of riding on a steed, a typical illusion of the witches' ride to the sabbat.

If Harner's explanation is correct, then most of the "genuine" sabbat meetings involved hallucinogenic experiences. The ointment was always applied *before* the witches went to the sabbat, never after they got there. So that whatever lay behind the papal decision to use the Inquisition to extirpate witchcraft, it could not have been the growing popularity of sabbats. What might have happened, of course, is that more people began "tripping." I won't rule out that possibility. But the Inquisition was not at all concerned with identifying witches on the basis of their possession of ointments (*The Hammer of the Witches* has little to say on the subject). It seems to me likely, therefore, that most of the "genuine" witches—the habitual trippers—were never identified, and that most of the people who were burned had never tripped.

Hallucinogenic ointments account for many of the specific features of witchcraft belief. Torture accounts for the spread of these beliefs far beyond the orbit of the actual users of the ointments. But there still remains the riddle of why five hundred thousand people had to die for crimes they committed in someone else's dreams.

The Great
Witch Craze

MOST PEOPLE don't know that military-messianic uprisings were as common in Europe from the thirteenth to the seventeenth centuries as they had been in Palestine in Greek and Roman times. Nor that the Protestant Reformation was in many ways the culmination or by-product of this messianic unrest. As was true of their predecessors in Palestine, outbreaks of messianic fervor in Europe were directed against the monopoly of wealth and power held by the governing classes. My explanation of the witchcraft craze is that it was largely created and sustained by the governing classes as a means of surpressing this wave of Christian messianism.

It is no accident that witchcraft came into increasing prominence along with violent messianic protests against social and economic inequities. The Pope gave permission to use torture against witches shortly before the Protestant Reformation, and the witch craze peaked during the sixteenth- and seventeenth-century wars and revolutions that put an end to the era of Christian unity.

For the European masses, the passing of feudalism and the emergence of strong national monarchies was a period of great stress. The development of trade, markets, and banking forced the owners of land and capital into enterprises aimed at maximizing profits. This could be done only by breaking up the small-scale paternalistic relationships characteristic of the feudal manorial estates and castle towns. Land holdings were divided, serfs and retainers were replaced by peasant renters and sharecroppers, and self-contained manors were converted into cash-crop agribusinesses. Country folk lost their subsistence plots and family homesteads, and great numbers of dispossessed peasants drifted to the towns, where they sought employment as wage laborers. From the eleventh century on, life became more competitive, impersonal, and commercialized—ruled by profit rather than tradition.

As the pauperization and alienation increased, more and more people began to make predictions about Christ's second coming. Many saw the end of the world unfolding before their eyes in the sin and luxury of the Church, the polarization of wealth, famines and plagues, the expansion of Islam, and the incessant wars between rival factions of the European nobility.

The foremost theoretician of Western European messianism was Joachim of Fiore, whose prophetic system has been called by historian Norman Cohn, "the most influential one known to Europe until the appearance of Marxism." Sometime between 1190 and 1195 Joachim, who was a Calabrian abbot, discovered how to calculate when the present world of suffering would give way to the kingdom of the spirit. Joachim believed that the first age of the world was the Age of the Father, the second the Age of the Son, the third the

Age of the Holy Spirit. The third age was to be the Sabbath or resting time, when there would be no need for wealth or property, labor, food or shelter; existence would be pure spirit and all material requirements would be superfluous. Hierarchical institutions such as the state and the Church would be replaced by a free community of perfect beings. Joachim predicted that the Age of the Spirit would begin by the year 1260. This date became the target of several military-messianic movements based on the belief that Emperor Frederick II (1194–1250) was going to usher in the Third Age.

Frederick openly defied the power of the Pope, causing his kingdom to be placed under a papal interdict prohibiting baptism, marriage, confession, and the other sacraments. Supporting Frederick was the fanatic poverty wing of the Franciscan order, known as the Spirituals. They claimed that Frederick would soon perform the role of Antichrist, purging the Church of wealth and luxury and destroying the clergy. In Germany, Frederick was proclaimed Savior by wandering Joachite preachers, who denounced the Pope and administered sacraments and granted absolution in defiance of the papal interdiction. In Swabia, one of these preachers, Brother Arnold, said that Christ would return in 1260 and confirm the fact that the Pope was Antichrist, and the clergy the "limbs" of Antichrist. They all would be condemned for living in luxury and exploiting and oppressing the poor. Frederick II would then confiscate the great wealth of Rome and distribute it to the poor—the only true Christians.

Frederick's untimely death in 1250 did not destroy the messianic fantasies asociated with his rule. He became a "Sleeping Emperor," and in 1284 a man who claimed to be the reawakened Frederick attracted followers in Neuss before he was burned for heresy. Savior Fredericks were still being burned hundreds of years later.

Norman Cohn describes a military-messianic document known as the *Book of a Hundred Chapters,* written at the beginning of the sixteenth century, which predicted that Frederick was coming on a white horse to rule the whole world. The clergy from the Pope on down would be annihilated at the rate of 2,300 persons per day. The emperor would also massacre all moneylenders, price-fixing merchants, and unscrupulous lawyers. All wealth would be appropriated and turned over to the poor; private property would be abolished, and all things would be held in common: "All property shall become one single property, then there will indeed be one shepherd and one sheepfold."

In preparation for the third age predicted by Joachim of Fiore, bands of men who specialized in beating themselves with iron-tipped thongs began to march from town to town. Arriving in a town square, these "flagellants" would strip to the waist and whip themselves on the back until the blood ran. The flagellants were initially concerned with penitence as a means of "straightening the path" for the third age. But their activities became increasingly subversive and anti-clerical, especially in Germany after 1260. When they began to claim that the mere act of participating in one of their processions absolved a man from sin, the Church declared them heretics and they were forced to go underground. They surfaced in 1348 as the Black Death swept across Europe. The flagellants blamed the Black Death on the Jews and incited mobs in town after town to massacre the Jewish inhabitants. Setting themselves above Pope and clergy, they claimed that their blood had the power of redemption and that they were an army of saints saving the world from God's wrath. They stoned the priests who tried to stop them, disrupted regular church services, and confiscated and redistributed church property.

The flagellant movement culminated in a messianic revolt led by one Konrad Schmid, who claimed to be the God-Emperor Frederick. Schmid whipped his followers and bathed them in their own blood as a higher form of baptism. Like New Guinea believers in cargo, the people of Thuringia sold their possessions, refused to work, and prepared to take their places in the angelic choir that would stand closest to the Emperor God after the Last Judgment. This event was set for 1369. Due to the energetic intervention of the Inquisition, Schmid was burned before he could complete his work. Years later, flagellants were still being discovered in Thuringia, and three hundred were burned in a single day in 1416.

One way to get rid of the troublemaking alienated poor was to enlist their aid in the Holy Wars, or Crusades, aimed at recapturing Jerusalem from Islam. Several of these Crusades backfired and turned into messianic revolutionary movements directed against the clergy and the nobility. In the Crusade of the Shepherds, for example, a renegade monk named Jacob claimed that he had received a letter from the Virgin Mary summoning all shepherds to free the Holy Sepulcher. Tens of thousands of poor people followed Jacob about, armed with pitchforks, hatchets, and daggers which they would hold aloft as they entered a town, intimidating the authorities so that they would be given a proper reception. Jacob had visions, healed the sick, gave miraculous banquets in which food appeared faster than it could be eaten, denounced the clergy, and killed anyone who dared to interrupt his sermons. His followers went from town to town, striking down the clergy or drowning them in the river.

The interplay among the essentially conservative but conflicting interests of the Church and the state and the threat of radical lower-class revolution drove Europe steadily closer to the Protestant Reformation. How this process worked can be seen in the Hussite movement of fifteenth-century Bohemia.

The Hussites confiscated church property and tried to compel the clergy to live a life of apostolic poverty. In retaliation, the Pope and his allies initiated a series of repressive campaigns now known as the Hussite Wars. As the violence spread, a third group of combatants emerged out of the pauperized masses. They were known as the Taborites—after Tabor on the Mount of Olives, where Jesus foretold his second coming. To the Taborites, the Hussite Wars were the beginning of the end of the world. They rushed into battle in order to "wash their hands in blood," led by messianic prophets who insisted that every true priest was under the obligation to pursue, wound, and kill every sinner. After exterminating the enemy, the Taborites expected Joachim de Fiore's third age to begin. There would be the usual lack of physical suffering or physical want; a community of love and peace, without taxes, property, or social classes. In 1419 thousands of these Bohemian "free spirits" (the originators of bohemianism as a lifestyle) established a commune near the town of Usti on the Luzhnica River. They supported themselves by forays into the countryside, stripping and looting anything they could get their hands on because as men of the Law of God, they felt they were entitled to take whatever belonged to the enemies of God.

Similar movements recurred in Germany throughout the fifteenth century. For example, in 1476 a shepherd named Hans Böhm had a vision of the Virgin Mary. He was told that henceforth the poor should refuse all payment of taxes and tithes in preparation for the coming kingdom. All people would soon be living together without distinction of rank; everyone would be given equal access to woods, water, pasture, and fishing and hunting areas. Crowds of pilgrims advanced on Niklashausen from all over Germany to see the "Holy Youth." They marched in long columns, greeted each other as "brother and sister," and sang revolutionary songs.

The specific form ultimately achieved by the Protestant Reformation cannot be understood apart from the radical military-messianic alternative which frightened the secular powers as much as it frightened the church. Like so many before him, Luther was convinced that he was living in the Last Days, that the Pope was Antichrist, and that the papacy would have to be destroyed before the Kingdom of God could be realized. But Luther's Kingdom of God would not be of this world; and he felt that preaching rather than armed revolt was the proper way to bring it about. The German nobility welcomed Luther's mixture of radical piety and conservative politics. It was the right combination for throwing off papal rule without increasing the risk of social upheaval.

Thomas Müntzer, originally a disciple of Luther, supplied the radical counterpoint to Luther's movement. Luther and Müntzer chose opposite sides in the great peasant revolt of 1525. Luther condemned the peasants in his pamphlet

"Against the Murdering, Thieving Hordes of Peasants," to which Müntzer replied that the people who supported Luther were themselves "robbers who use the law to forbid others to rob." Müntzer insisted that what Luther called God's law was simply a device for protecting property. The "seed-grounds of usury and theft and robbery are our Lords and Princes." He accused Luther of strengthening the power of the "ungodly scoundrels, so that they shall continue in their old ways." Convinced that the peasant uprising was the beginning of the New Kingdom, Müntzer took over command of the peasant army. He compared his role to that of Gideon in the battle with the Midianites, and on the eve of encountering the enemy, he told his ill-equipped and untrained peasant followers that God had spoken to him and had promised victory. He said that he himself would protect them by catching the cannonballs in his sleeve. God would never allow his chosen people to perish. With the first cannonades, the peasants broke rank and 5,000 were slaughtered while running away. Müntzer himself was tortured and then beheaded some time later.

The radical wing of the Reformation continued in full force during the sixteenth and early part of the seventeenth centuries. Known as the Anabaptist movement, it gave rise to at least forty different sects and dozens of military-messianic uprisings in the Taborite and Müntzer tradition, and was widely regarded by Catholic and Protestant rulers alike as an omnipresent heretical conspiracy to overthrow all property relations and redistribute the wealth of Church and state among the poor. For example, one of Müntzer's disciples, Hans Hut, announced that Christ would return in 1528 to inaugurate the kingdom of God, with free love and community of goods. The Anabaptists would judge the false priests and pastors. Kings, nobles, and the great ones of the earth would be cast into chains. Melchoir Hoffman, another follower of Müntzer, predicted that the world would end in 1533. Hoffman was succeeded by a baker, Jan Matthys of Haarlem, who preached that the righteous must take up the sword and actively prepare the way for Christ by cleansing the earth of the ungodly. In 1534 Münster, Westphalia, became the center of the Anabaptist movement. All Catholics and Protestants were evicted, and private property was abolished. The leadership was soon taken over by John of Leyden, who claimed to be David's successor and who demanded royal honors and absolute obedience in what the Anabaptists called their "New Jerusalem."

During the seventeenth century in England similar radical messianic motifs animated the lower classes, providing much of the energy for the English Civil War. Oliver Cromwell's New Model Army contained thousands of volunteers who believed that a kingdom of "Saints" would be established on English soil and that Christ would descend to rule over them. In 1649 Gerrard Winstanley received a vision commanding him to prepare for the end of the world by establishing a community of "Diggers," in which private property, class distinction, and all forms of coercion would have no place. And in 1656 Cromwell's erstwhile supporters, the Fifth Monarchy Men, declared him Antichrist, and tried to set up a kingdom of the Saints by force of arms—Fifth Monarchy referring to the millennium when Christ would reign for 1,000 years.

• • •

What has all this to do with witchcraft? As I indicated at the beginning of the chapter, there is a close chronological relationship between the onset of the witch craze and the development of European messianism. Institor and Sprenger's witch-hunting system was approved by Innocent VIII at a time when Europe was bubbling to the brim with third-age prophecies and messianic movements. The witch mania reached its peak in the aftermath of the Reformation—both Luther and Calvin were ardent believers in the dangers of witchcraft—and so did the violent radical protest movements based on revolutionary third-age messianic doctrines.

Is there a practical explanation for the parallel development of messianic social protest and the witchcraft craze? One conventional point of view is that witchcraft itself was a form of social protest. For example, according to Professor Jeffrey Burton Russell—who is an expert on the history of medieval dissent—witchcraft, mysticism, the flagellants, and popular heresy all belong in the same category. "All, to one degree or another, were rejections of an institutional structure that was found wanting."

I disagree. To explain the witch craze as social protest, you have to go pretty far toward adopting the view of "reality" set forth in *The Hammer of the Witches*. You have to believe that Europe was infested with great numbers of people who threatened the status quo by gathering together to worship the devil. But if the real flying witches were mainly henbane trippers, they don't belong in the same category as the Taborites or the Anabaptists any more than junkies belong with Black Panthers. A few people here and there hallucinating about intercourse with the Devil, or casting spells on some neighbor's cow, were not a threat to the survival of the propertied and governing classes. Witches were probably drawn from the ranks of frustrated and discontented people; but this does not make witches subversive. For a movement to be a serious protest against an established order it must either have explicit doctrines of social criticism, or it must be launched on a dangerous or threatening course of action. Whatever the witches did at their sabbats, if they ever got there at all, there is no evidence that they spent their time condemning the luxury of the Church or calling for the abolition of private property and the end of distinctions of rank and authority. If they did, they weren't witches but Waldensians, Taborites, Anabaptists, or members of some other radical politico-religious sect—many of whom were undoubtedly burned for witchcraft rather than for their messianic beliefs.

To understand the witch craze, we must be willing to identify a species of reality that is separate from, and opposed to, the lifestyle consciousness of both the witches and the inquisitors. For Professor Russell, it is sufficient that the clergy and the nobility *thought* witchcraft was dangerous and subversive. "What people thought happened," he says, "is as interesting as what 'objectively' did happen, and much more certain." But this is precisely the point made by Institor and Sprenger: you are responsible for what you do in someone else's dreams!

We have to make up our minds about certain events. Else Gwinner did not have intercourse with the Devil, and that is not an uninteresting or uncertain conclusion considering the fact that she was carbonized for having done it.

As in the case of each of the seemingly bizarre lifestyles that I have taken up so far, the witch craze can't be explained in terms of the consciousness of the people who participated in it. Everything hinges on the observer's readiness to indulge or oppose the fantasies of the various participants.

If witchcraft was dangerous heresy, as the Inquisition insisted, there is no mystery about why the Inquisition should have become obsessed with suppressing it. If, on the other hand, witchcraft was a relatively harmless, if not largely hallucinatory, activity, why was there so much effort spent on suppressing it—especially when the Church was being pushed to the limits of its resources by the great military-messianic upsurge of the fifteenth century?

This leads to a crucial question concerning what happened as distinct from what people thought happened. Is it true that the Inquisition was devoted to the suppression of the witch heresy? The assumption that the main business of the witch hunters was the annihilation of witches rests on the professed lifestyle consciousness of the inquisitors. But the contrary assumption—namely, that the witch hunters went out of their way to increase the supply of witches and to spread the belief that witches were real, omnipresent, and dangerous—rests on very solid evidence. Why should modern scholars accept the premises of the inquisitor's lifestyle consciousness? The situation demands that we ask not why the inquisitors were obsessed with destroying witchcraft, but rather why they were so obsessed with creating it. Regardless of what they or their victims may have intended, the inevitable effect of the inquisitorial system was to make witchcraft more believable, and hence to increase the number of witchcraft accusations.

The witch-hunt system was too well designed, too enduring, too grim and stubborn. It could only have been sustained by interests that were equally enduring, grim, and stubborn. The witchcraft system and the witch craze had practical and mundane uses apart from the stated goals of the witch hunters. I am not referring here to the emoluments and petty advantages which I described earlier—the confiscation of property and the fees charged for torture and execution. These rewards help to explain why the technicians of the witch hunt went about their work with lively enthusiasm. But such benefits were part of the apparatus of witch-hunting rather than one of its causes.

I suggest that the best way to understand the cause of the witch mania is to examine its earthly results rather than its heavenly intentions. The principal result of the witch-hunt system (aside from charred bodies) was that the poor came to believe that they were being victimized by witches and devils instead of princes and popes. Did your roof leak, your cow abort, your oats wither, your wine go sour, your head ache, your baby die? It was a neighbor, the one who broke your fence, owed you money, or wanted your land—a neighbor turned witch. Did the price of bread go up, taxes soar, wages fall, jobs grow scarce? It was the work of the witches. Did plague and famine carry off a third of the inhabitants of every village and town? The diabolical, infernal witches were growing bolder all the time. Against the people's phantom enemies, Church and state mounted a bold campaign. The authorities were unstinting in their efforts to ward off this evil, and rich and poor alike could be thankful for the energy and bravery displayed in the battle.

The practical significance of the witch mania therefore was that it shifted responsibility for the crisis of late medieval society from both Church and state to imaginary demons in

237

human form. Preoccupied with the fantastic activities of these demons, the distraught, alienated, pauperized masses blamed the rampant Devil instead of the corrupt clergy and the rapacious nobility. Not only were the Church and state exonerated, but they were made indispensable. The clergy and nobility emerged as the great protectors of mankind against an enemy who was omnipresent but difficult to detect. Here at last was a reason to pay tithes and obey the tax collector. Vital services pertaining to this life rather than the next were being carried out with sound and fury, flame and smoke. You could actually see the authorities doing something to make life a little more secure; you could actually hear the witches scream as they went down to hell.

Who were the scapegoats? H. C. Erik Midelfort's unique study of 1,258 witchcraft executions in southwestern Germany during the period 1562 to 1684 shows that 82 percent of the witches were females. Defenseless old women and lower-class midwives were usually the first to be accused in any local outbreak. As additional names were wrung from the first victims, children of both sexes, and men, began to figure more prominently. During the culminating panic phase characterized by mass executions, innkeepers, a few wealthy merchants, and an occasional magistrate and teacher would be put to death. But as the flames licked closer to the names of people who enjoyed high rank and power, the judges lost confidence in the confessions and the panics ceased. Doctors, lawyers, and university professors were seldom threatened. Evidently the inquisitors themselves and the clergy in general were also quite safe. If on occasion some poor bewildered soul was foolish enough to have seen the bishop or the crown prince at a recent sabbat, she surely brought upon herself tortures beyond recounting. Small wonder that Midelfort could find only three instances of accusations of witchcraft against members of the nobility, and not one of those so accused was executed.

Far from being "the reflection of an institutional structure that was found wanting," the witch mania was an integral part of the defense of that institutional structure. This can best be seen by comparing the witch mania with its contemporary antithesis, military messianism. The witch mania and the military-messianic movements both incorporated popular religious themes that were partially endorsed by the established Church. They both built upon the existing lifestyle consciousness, but with totally different consequences. Military messianism brought the poor and the dispossessed together. It gave them a sense of collective mission, diminished social distance, made them feel like "brother and sister." It mobilized people over whole regions, focused their energies upon a particular time and place, and led to pitched battles between the propertyless and pauperized masses and the people who were at the top of the social pyramid. The witchcraft mania, on the other hand, dispersed and fragmented all the latent energies of protest. It demobilized the poor and the dispossessed, increased their social distance, filled them with mutual suspicions, pitted neighbor against neighbor, isolated everyone, made everyone fearful, heightened everyone's insecurity, made everyone feel helpless and dependent on the governing classes, gave everyone's anger and frustration a purely local focus. In so doing, it drew the poor further and further away from confronting the ecclesiastical and secular establishment with demands for the redistribution of wealth and the leveling of rank. The witch mania was radical military messianism in reverse. It was the magic bullet of society's privileged and powerful classes. That was its secret.

Return
of the Witch

After being branded as superstition and suffering years of ridicule, witchcraft has returned as a respectable source of titillation. Not only witchcraft, but all kinds of occult and mystical specialties, ranging from astrology to Zen and including meditation, Hare Krishna, and the *I Ching*, an ancient Chinese system of magic. Catching the spirit of the times, a textbook titled *Modern Cultural Anthropology* recently won instant success by declaring: "Human freedom includes the freedom to believe."

The unexpected resurgence of attitudes and theories long held to be incompatible with the expansion of Western science and technology is associated with the development of a lifestyle which has been given the name "counter-culture." According to Theodore Roszak, one of the movement's adult prophets, counter-culture will save the world from the "myths of objective consciousness." It will "subvert the scientific world view" and substitute a new culture in which the "non-intellective capacities" will reign supreme.

Charles A. Reich, another minor prophet of recent years, speaks of a millennial state of mind which he calls Consciousness III. To achieve Consciousness III is "to be deeply suspicious of logic, rationality, analysis, and of principles."

In the lifestyle of the counter-culture, feelings, spontaneity, imagination are good; science, logic, objectivity are bad. Its members boast of fleeing "objectivity" as if from a place inhabited by plague.

A central aspect of counter-culture is the belief that consciousness controls history. People are what goes on in their minds; to make them better, all you have to do is give them better ideas. Objective conditions count for little. The entire world is to be altered as a result of a "revolution in consciousness." All we need do to stop crime, end poverty, beautify cities, eliminate war, live in peace and harmony with ourselves and nature, is to open our minds to Consciousness III. "Consciousness is prior to structure . . . The whole corporate state rests on nothing but consciousness."

In the counter-culture, consciousness is stimulated and made aware of its untapped potential. Counter-culture people take journeys—"head trips"—to broaden their minds. They use pot, LSD, or mushrooms "to get their heads together." They rap, encounter, or chant in order to "freak out" with Jesus, Buddha, Mao Tse-tung.

The aim is to express consciousness, demonstrate consciousness, alter consciousness, raise consciousness, expand consciousness—anything but objectify consciousness. To the Aquarian, mind-blown, stoned, freaked-out partisans of Consciousness III, reason is an invention of the military-industrial complex. It should be "offed" like any other "pig."

Psychedelic drugs are useful because they allow "illogical"

relationships to seem "perfectly natural." They are good because, in Reich's words, they make "*unreal* what society takes most seriously: time schedules, rational connections, competition, anger, excellence, authority, private property, law, status, the primacy of the state." They are a "truth serum that repeals false consciousness." One who has achieved Consciousness III "does not 'know the facts.' He doesn't have to because he still 'knows' the truth that seems hidden from others."

Counter-culture celebrates the supposedly natural life of primitive peoples. Its members wear beads, headbands, body paint, and colorful tattered clothing; they yearn to be a tribe. They seem to believe that tribal peoples are nonmaterialistic, spontaneous, and reverently in touch with occult sources of enchantment.

In the anthropology of counter-culture, primitive consciousness is epitomized by the shaman, a figure who has light and power but never pays electric bills. Shamans are admired because they are adept at "cultivating exotic states of awareness" and at roving "among the hidden powers of the universe." The shaman possesses "superconsciousness." He has "eyes of fire that burn through the ordinariness of the world and perceive the wonders and terrors beyond." Using hallucinogens and other techniques such as self-asphyxiation, and hypnotic drums and dance rhythms, the shaman, according to Roszak, "cultivates his rapport with the non-intellective sources of the personality as assiduously as any scientist trains himself to objectivity."

There is much to be learned about the counter-culture from a consideration of Carlos Castaneda's popular hero Don Juan, a mysterious superconscious Yaqui Indian "man of knowledge." Castaneda writes of his experiences as a fledgling anthropology student who wanted to penetrate the separate, nonordinary reality of the shaman's world. Don Juan accepted Castaneda as an apprentice, and Castaneda set out to write a doctoral dissertation based on Don Juan's teachings. To remake Castaneda into a "man of knowledge," Don Juan introduced the innocent student to various hallucinogenic substances. After encountering a transparent luminescent dog and a hundred-foot gnat, Castaneda began to doubt that his normal reality was any more real than the nonordinary reality to which his mentor had conducted him. At the outset, Castaneda was intent on finding out how a "man of knowledge" conceives of the world. But the apprentice gradually began to feel that he was learning something about the world itself.

"It is stupid and wasteful," noted another anthropologist, Paul Riesman, in a *New York Times* book review, "to think of Don Juan's knowledge—and that of other non-Western peoples—as no more than a conception of some fixed reality. Castaneda makes it clear that the teachings of Don Juan do tell us something of how the world really is."

Wrong on both counts. Castaneda does not make anything clear. And Don Juan's "separate reality" is not unfamiliar to "Western peoples."

Castaneda's most famous hallucinogenic trip is very reminiscent of matters I discussed here earlier. Don Juan and Castaneda spent several days preparing a paste from *yerba del diablo*—"devil's weed"—mixed with lard and other ingredients. Under Don Juan's supervision, the apprentice spread the paste on the soles of his feet and up the insides of his legs, reserving the largest part for his genitals. The paste had a suffocating, pungent smell—"like a gas of some sort." Castaneda straightened up and started to walk, but his legs felt "rubbery and long, extremely long."

I looked down and saw Don Juan sitting below me; way below me. The momentum carried me forward one more step, which was even more elastic and longer than the preceding one. And from there I soared. I remember coming down once; then I pushed up with both feet, sprang backwards and glided on my back. I saw the dark sky above me, the clouds going by me. I jerked my body so I could look down. I saw the dark mass of the mountains. My speed was extraordinary.

After learning how to maneuver by turning his head, Castaneda experienced "such freedom and swiftness as he had never known before." At last he felt obliged to descend. It was morning and he was naked and a half-mile from where he had set out. Don Juan assured him that with practice he would become a better flyer:

You can soar through the air for hundreds of miles to see what is happening at any place you want, or to deliver a fatal blow to your enemies far away.

Castaneda asked his teacher, "Did I really fly, Don Juan?" and the shaman replied, "That's what you told me. Didn't you?"

Then I really didn't fly, Don Juan. I flew in my imagination, in my mind alone. Where was my body?

To which Don Juan rejoined:

You don't think a man flies; and yet a *brujo* [witch] can move a thousand miles in one second to see what is going on. He can deliver a blow to his enemies long distances away. So does he or doesn't he fly?

Does this sound familiar? It should. What are Don Juan and Castaneda debating if not the respective merits of the Canon Episcopi and Institor and Sprenger's *Hammer of the Witches?* Does the witch fly in mind alone or in body also? At last, Castaneda asks Don Juan what would happen if he tied himself to a rock with a heavy chain: "I'm afraid you will have to fly holding the rock with its heavy chain."

As we learned from Professor Harner, European witches flew after rubbing themselves with salves and unguents containing the skin-penetrating alkaloid atropine. Professor Harner also informs us that atropine is an active ingredient in the *Datura* genus of plants, known in the New World as Jimson weed, thorn apple, Gabriel's trumpet, mad apple, and devil's weed—the last being the variety whose root made Castaneda airborne. In fact, Harner predicted that Castaneda would fly like a witch before Castaneda rubbed himself with devil's weed:

Several years ago I ran across a reference to the use of a *Datura* ointment by the Yaqui Indians of Northern Mexico, who reportedly rubbed it on the stomach "to see visions." I called this to the attention of my colleague and friend, Carlos Castaneda, who was studying under a Yaqui shaman, and asked him to find out if the Yaqui used the ointment for flying and to determine its effects.

So shamanistic superconsciousness is the consciousness of witches favorably regarded in a world no longer threatened by the Inquisition. The "separate reality" previously unknown to smugly objective "Western peoples" is so much a part of Western civilization that a scant three hundred years ago "objectifiers" were burned at the stake for denying that witches could fly.

In the first chapter, I cited the claim that the expansion of "objective consciousness" inevitably results in a loss of "moral sensibility." Counter-culture and Consciousness III represent themselves as humanizing trends concerned with the restoration of sentiment, compassion, love, and mutual trust in human relationshops. I find it difficult to reconcile this moral posture with the interest expressed in witchcraft and shamanism. Don Juan, for instance, can only be described as amoral. He may know how to "rove among the hidden powers of the universe," but he is not troubled by the difference between good and evil in the traditional Western sense of morality. His teachings are, in fact, devoid of "moral sensibility."

One incident in Castaneda's second book epitomizes the moral opacity of the shaman's superconsciousness more than any other. Having achieved fame and fortune with *The Teachings of Don Juan,* Castaneda tried to find his mentor to give him a copy. While waiting for Don Juan to appear, Castaneda studied a pack of street urchins who lived by eating scraps left on the tables in his hotel. After three days of watching the children darting in and out "like vultures," Castaneda became "truly despondent." Don Juan was surprised to hear this. "Do you really feel sorry for them?" he wanted to know. Castaneda insisted that he did, and Don Juan asked him, "Why?"

Because I'm concerned with the well-being of my fellow men. Those are children and their world is ugly and cheap.

Castaneda does not say that he feels sorry for the children because they are eating the scraps he has left on the table. What seems to bother him is that their lives are "ugly and cheap." Hunger and poverty give rise to bad thoughts, or bad dreams. Taking the cue, Don Juan admonished his pupil for supposing that such waifs could not mature mentally and become "men of knowledge":

Do you think that your very rich world would ever help you to become a man of knowledge?

When Castaneda is forced to admit that his affluence hasn't helped him to become a successful witch, Don Juan nails him:

Then how can you feel sorry for those children? . . . Any of them could become a man of knowledge. All the men of knowledge I know were kids like those you saw eating leftovers and licking tables.

For many members of the counter-culture, the morally most degenerate product of the scientific world view is the technocrat—the heartless, inscrutable technician devoted to expert knowledge, but indifferent as to who uses it and for what end. Yet Don Juan is precisely such a technocrat. The knowledge he imparts to Castaneda carries no moral burden. In becoming a "man of knowledge," Castaneda's main concern is to avoid taking something that will flip him into a permanent orbit. For all the moral concern about how Don Juan's extraordinary powers are to be applied, Castaneda might as well have learned how to pilot a B-52. His relationship to Don Juan unfolds in a moral wasteland in which technology is the supreme good, even if he and his teacher eat "buttons" instead of pressing them.

Return of the Witch

I contend that it is quite impossible to subvert objective knowledge without subverting the basis of moral judgments. If we cannot know with reasonable certainty who did what, when, and where, we can scarcely hope to render a moral account of ourselves. Not being able to distinguish between criminal and victim, rich and poor, exploiter and exploited, we must either advocate the total suspension of moral judgments, or adopt the inquisitorial position and hold people responsible for what they do in each other's dreams.

As *Time* magazine reporters discovered while trying to do a story on Carlos Castaneda, Consciousness III can cast an impenetrable fog over the simplest human events. Invoking his freedom of belief, Castaneda either fabricated, imagined, or hallucinated extensive portions of his own biography:

> Born in Peru, not Brazil
> Date of birth 1925, not 1935
> Mother died when he was 6, not 24
> Father a jeweler, not a professor of literature
> Studied painting and sculpture in Lima, not Milan

"To ask me to verify my life by giving you my statistics," said Castaneda, "is like using science to validate sorcery. It robs the world of its magic."

According to Castaneda, Don Juan is the same way. The world's most famous shaman doesn't want to be photographed, tape-recorded, or questioned, even by his apprentice. No one except Castaneda appears to know who Don Juan is. Castaneda freely admits: "Oh, I'm a bullshitter! Oh, how I love to throw the bull around"; at least one friend from Peru remembers him as a "big liar."

Don Juan may not exist. Or perhaps we should say Casta-

251

neda met a Yaqui witch in "mind" but not in "body." On the authority of the Inquisition, this might still have resulted in an accurate account of Don Juan's teachings. Or, perhaps, Castaneda went sometimes in "imagination" and other times in "body." These are intriguing ideas, but they can make only an imaginary contribution to the improvement of anyone's moral sensibilities.

Counter-culture makes claims that extend far beyond the supposed preservation of individual morality. Its advocates insist that superconsciousness can make the world into a more friendly and more habitable place; they see flight from objectivity as a politically effective way to achieve an equitable distribution of wealth, recycling of resources, abolition of impersonal bureaucracies, and the correction of other dehumanizing aspects of modern technocratic societies. These ills allegedly come from the bad ideas we have about status and work. If we stop trying to show off, and if we stop believing that work is a good thing in itself, revolutionary transformation will occur without the need for anyone to get hurt. As in fairyland, "we can make a new choice whenever we are ready to do so." Capitalism, the corporate state, the age of science, the Protestant ethic—all represent types of consciousness, and they can be altered by choosing a new consciousness. "All we have to do is close our eyes and imagine that everyone has become a Consciousness III: The Corporate State vanishes . . . The power of the Corporate State will be ended as miraculously as a kiss breaks a witch's evil enchantment."

Consciousness so far out of touch with practical and mundane constraints is, in fact, witchcraft rather than politics. People can change their consciousness whenever they want to. But people usually don't want to. Consciousness is adapted to practical and mundane conditions. These conditions cannot be imagined into or out of existence the way a shaman makes hundred-foot gnats appear and disappear. As I pointed out earlier in the chapter on potlatch, prestige systems are not created by vibrations from outer space. People learn the consciousness of competitive consumerism because they are constrained to do so by immensely powerful political and economic forces. These forces can be modified only by practical activities aimed at changing consciousness by changing the material conditions of consciousness.

Counter-culture's glad tidings of revolution by consciousness are neither new nor revolutionary. Christianity has been trying to achieve a revolution by consciousness for two thousand years. Who would deny that Christian consciousness *could* have changed the world? Yet it was the world that changed Christian consciousness. If everybody adopted a peaceful, loving, generous, noncompetitive lifestyle, we could have something better than counter-culture—we could have the Kingdom of God.

Politics conceived in the image of Consciousness III takes place in the mind, not the body. The convenience of this form of politics to those who already possess wealth and power should be obvious. To reflect philosophically that poverty is, after all, a state of mind has always been a source of comfort for those who are not poor. In this regard, counter-culture merely brings forward in slightly modified form the traditional contempt expressed by Christian theorists for worldly possessions. Also traditional and within the mainstream of conservative politics is the guarantee that nothing will happen by force. Consciousness III will destroy the corporate state "without violence, without seizure of political power, without overthrow of any existing group of people." Counter-culture is sworn to attack minds, not capital gains or depletion allowances.

By definition, counter-culture is the lifestyle of alienated middle-class college-educated youth. Specifically excluded are those who "continue to tend the ashes of the proletarian revolution" and "the militant black young." The hope that counter-culture will transform society into "something a human being can identify as home" rests on the fact that it is a middle-class movement. What makes it so important "is that a radical rejection of science and technological values should appear so close to the center of our society, rather than on the negligible margins. It is the middle-class young who are conducting this politics of consciousness."

Aside from the question of whether a politics of pure consciousness should be called politics rather than witchcraft or some other form of magic, two other dubious points should be noted. First, counter-culture does not reject technological values *in toto*; second, the rejection of a certain kind of science has always been present at the very center of our civilization.

Counter-culture is not averse to making use of the technological products of "objective" scientific research. Telephones, FM stations, solid-state stereos, cheap jet flights, estrogen birth-control pills, and chemical hallucinogens and antidotes are essential to the good life of Consciousness III.

Moreover, dependence on high-decibel high-fidelity music has created the greatest degree of subordination of a popular idiom to technology in the history of the performing arts. At least tacitly, therefore, counter-culture accepts the existence of specialists in the physical and biological sciences whose job it is to design and maintain the lifestyle's technological infrastructure.

The most hated forms of science in the perspective of Consciousness III are not the laboratory sciences, but those which seek to apply laboratory standards to the study of history and lifestyles. Counter-culture depicts the turning away from the scientific study of lifestyles and history as if it were a departure from some deeply ingrained pattern. But even among so-called behavioral and social scientists, the prevailing form of knowledge is not and *never has been* what the counter-culture says it is. How can anyone react to an overdose of the science of lifestyles when the science of lifestyles insists that the riddles examined in the previous chapters of this book have no scientific explanation? Extensive "objectification" in the study of lifestyle phenomena is nothing but a myth of the social dreamwork of the counter-culture. The prevailing consciousness among the majority of professionals concerned with explaining lifestyle phenomena is virtually indistinguishable from Consciousness III.

If the return of the witch involved turning the physics, chemistry, and biology labs over to people who disdain objective evidence and rational analysis, we would have little to fear. The exercise of the freedom of belief in the laboratory could only be a temporary inconvenience until the charred remains of superconscious experimenters were swept out along with the rubble they created. Unfortunately, obscurantism applied to lifestyles does not self-destruct. Doctrines that prevent people from understanding the causes of their social existence have great social value. In a society dominated by inequitable modes of production and exchange, lifestyle studies that obscure and distort the nature of the social system are far more common and more highly valued than the mythological "objective" studies dreaded by the counter-culture. Obscurantism applied to lifestyle studies lacks the engineering "praxis" of the laboratory sciences. Falsifiers, mystics, and double-talkers do not get swept out with the rubble; in fact, there is no rubble because everything goes on just as it always did.

In previous chapters I have shown that profoundly mysti-fied consciousness is sometimes capable of galvanizing dis-sent into effective mass movements. We have seen how suc-cessive forms of messianism in Palestine, Europe, and Mel-anesia carried forward vast revolutionary impulses aimed at more equitable distributions of wealth and power. And we have also seen how the Renaissance Church and state used the witch craze to enchant and befuddle the communitarian radicals.

Where does counter-culture fit into this? Is it a conserva-tive or a radical force? In its own dreamwork, counter-culture identifies with the tradition of millenarian transformation. Theodore Roszak says the primary goal of counter-culture is to proclaim "a new heaven and a new earth," and in its formative phase, Consciousness III brought crowds of dis-senting youth together at rock concerts and antiwar protests. But even at the peak of its organizational efficiency, counter-culture lacked the fundamentals of messianism. It had no charismatic leaders and it lacked a vision of a well-defined moral order. In Consciousness III, leadership is another trick of the military-industrial complex, and as I indicated a mo-ment ago, a set of well-defined moral goals cannot be reconciled with the amoral relativism of shamans like Don Juan.

The flight from objectivity, amoral relativism, and acceptance of the omnipotence of thought speak of the witch and not the savior. Consciousness III has all the classic symptoms of a lifestyle dreamwork whose social function is to dissolve and fragment the energies of dissent. This should have been clear from the great importance given to "doing your own thing." You can't make a revolution if everybody does his own thing. To make a revolution, everybody must do the same thing.

So, the return of the witch is not a mere inscrutable bit of whimsy. The modern witchcraft revival has definite points of similarity with the late medieval craze. Of course there are many important differences. The modern witch is admired while the old witch is feared. No one in the counter-culture wants to burn anyone either for believing or disbelieving in witches; Reich and Roszak are not Institor and Sprenger; and the counter-culture fortunately has no commitment to any specific body of dogma. Yet we are left with the fact that the counter-culture and the Inquisition stand shoulder to shoulder on the issue of the witch's flight. Within counter-culture's freedom to believe, witches are once more as believable as anything else. This belief, for all its playful innocence, makes a definite contribution to the consolidation or stabilization of contemporary inequalities. Millions of educated youth seriously believe that the proposal to kiss away the corporate state as if it were an "evil enchantment" is no less effective or realistic than any other form of political consciousness. Like its medieval predecessor, our modern witch fad blunts and befuddles the forces of dissent. Like the rest of the counter-culture, it postpones the development of a rational set of political commitments. And that is why it is so popular among the more affluent segments of our population. That is why the witch has returned.

Epilogue

IF THE WITCH is here, can the savior be far behind?

A case has been made by Norman Cohn in his book *The Pursuit of the Millennium* for linking the messianic movements that preceded the Protestant Reformation with the secular convulsions of the twentieth century. Despite their contempt for the specific myths and legends of Judeo-Christian messianism, the lifestyle consciousness of figures like Lenin, Hitler, and Mussolini arose from a set of practical and mundane conditions similar to those responsible for the rise of such religious saviors as John of Leyden, Müntzer, and even—I would add—Manahem, Bar Kochva, and Yali. Secular, atheistic military messiahs share with their religious predecessors a "boundless, millennial promise made with boundless, prophet-like conviction." Like the Judeo-Christian saviors, they claim to be personally charged with the mission of bringing history to a preordained consummation. For Hitler it was to be the Thousand Year Reich purified of the polypus of the Jews and other in-dwelling witches and devils; for Lenin, it was to be the Communist Jerusalem whose motto was that of the first Christian commune: "And all that believed were together and had all things in common." Or as Trotsky put it: "Let the priests of all religious confessions tell of a paradise in the world beyond—we say we will create a true paradise for men on this earth." For the alienated, insecure, marginal, pauperized, bedeviled, and bewitched masses, the secular messiah promises redemption and fulfillment on a cosmic scale. Not only a chance to improve one's everyday existence, but total involvement in a mission of "stupendous, unique importance."

Measured by the grandiose visions of military-messianic consciousness, counter-culture appears to be a relatively harmless affirmation of the futility of political struggle, either of the right, left, or center. But complacency is an apt response to Consciousness III only in the short run and in the absence of any well-formed discipline capable of explaining the causal processes of history.

The intended "subversion of the scientific world view" is not dangerous because it actually threatens any part of the technological infrastructure of our civilization. Counter-culture enthusiasts are as dependent upon higher energy transport, solid-state electronics, and the mass production of textiles and food as the rest of us, and they lack both the will and the knowledge necessary for a reversion to more primitive forms of production and communication. At any rate, there is nothing to fear from any sect, class, or nation that fails to participate in the further advance of nuclear, cybernetic, and biophysical technology. Such groups will inevitably suffer the fate of the other Stone Age peoples of the twentieth century. They may survive, but only precariously and at the sufferance of immensely more powerful neighbors—on reservations or in communes protected for their value as tourist attractions. To regress to more primitive stages of technology, or even to hold the line at what the industrial powers now possess, cannot but appear as the most ludicrous and harebrained of proposals to the majority of mankind that grows daily more determined to improve their lives by breaking the Euro-American and Japanese monopoly on science and technology. A million chanting Reichs and Roszaks affect the advance and spread of science and technology about as much as the chirping of a single vagrant cricket affects the operation of an automated blast furnace. The threat of counterculture lies elsewhere.

The gurus of Consciousness III cannot conceivably halt or slow down the advance of technology; but they can increase the level of popular befuddlement concerning how that technology is to be made to reduce rather than intensify inequities and exploitation, how it is to be made to serve humane and constructive purposes rather than cause terror and destruction. The deepening confusion, psychic involution, and amorality epitomized in the return of the witch carry with them for anyone aware of the history of our civilization the imminent threat of the return of the messiah. Disdain of reason, evidence, and objectivity—superconsciousness and its heady freedom of belief—are steadily stripping an entire generation of the intellectual means of resisting the next call for a "final and decisive struggle" to achieve redemption and salvation on a cosmic scale.

Head trips and freak-outs cannot alter the material basis of exploitation and alienation. Consciousness III will change nothing that is fundamental or causative in the structure of capitalism or imperialism. What lies ahead, therefore, is not a do-it-yourself utopia, but some new and more malignant form of military messianism, brought on by the antics of a middle class that tried to tame its generals with telepathic messages and that thought it could humanize the greatest concentration of corporate wealth the world has ever seen by going barefoot and eating unhomogenized peanut butter.

As I said at the beginning of this book, the most pernicious fabrication perpetrated in the name of the freedom to believe is the contention that we are menaced by an overdose of "objectivity" about the causes of our own lifestyles. The lifestyle of groups such as the Yanomamo and Maring make clear what utter nonsense it is to suppose that scientific objectivity is humanity's original sin. It is evident from the history of Europe alone that the maiming, drawing and quartering, racking, hanging, drowning, crucifying, and burning of innocent people long antedate the rise of modern science and technology.

Some of the specific forms of inequity and alienation characteristic of industrial society are clearly products of the specific tools and techniques made available by advances in the natural and behavioral sciences. But none of the pathologies of contemporary life can be blamed on an overdose of scientific objectivity concerning the causes of lifestyle phenomena. Scientific objectivity about the fundamental causes of racism is not what keeps our ethnics at each others' throats, overturns school buses, and blocks the construction of apartments for underprivileged families. Scientific objectivity is not the cause of male, female, or homosexual chauvinism. It was not an overdose of scientific objectivity about lifestyles that produced the lopsided priorities that favor

264

moon landings and missiles over hospitals and houses. Nor is it an overdose of scientific objectivity about lifestyles that has created the population crisis. And what has scientific objectivity got to do with the infinite itch of consumerism, conspicuous consumption, conspicuous waste, built-in obsolescence, status hunger, the TV wasteland, and all the other weird driving forces of our competitive capitalist economy? Was it a lack of freedom of belief that led to the looting of minerals, forests, and soils, to the sewers running in the sky and the tarpits on the beaches? What was rational, reasonable, "objective," or "scientific" about all that? How does an overdose of objectivity about lifestyles explain a war that three Presidents couldn't give a rational reason for fighting but also couldn't stop?

One might as well believe that objectivity was the commanding lifestyle of Germany in 1932, that the Aryan beast cult of blond manhood, anathematization of the Semites, gypsies, and Slavs, worship of the fatherland, and the Wagnerian chanting, goose-stepping and *Sieg-Heiling* in front of *der Führer* all resulted from the atrophy of the "nonintellective capacities" and feelings of the German people. Ditto Stalinism with its Uncle Joe cult, genuflections before the corpse of Lenin, Kremlin intrigues, Siberian slave camps, and party-line dogmatism.

Of course we have our Strangelove zero-sum-game specialists, would-be super-objectifiers who objectify human life by counting corpses and computerizing death. But the moral flaw of such technologists and their political handlers is a shortage of scientific objectivity about the causes of lifestyle differences, not a surplus. The moral collapse of Vietnam was scarcely caused by an overdose of objective consciousness about what we were doing. It consisted of the failure to expand consciousness beyond mere instrumental tasks to the practical and banal significance of our national goals and policies. We kept the war going in Vietnam because our consciousness was mystified by symbols of patriotism, dreams of glory, unyielding pride, and visions of empire. In mood we were exactly what the counter-culture people want us to become. We imagined we were menaced by slant-eyed devils and worthless little yellow men; we enthralled ourselves with visions of our own ineffable majesty. In short, we were stoned.

I see no reason why the further indulgence of involuted, ethnocentric, irrational, and subjective modes of consciousness should result in anything markedly different from what we have always had: witches and messiahs. We don't need more weird vibrations, bigger psychotropic cults, and zanier head trips. I make no claim for the millenarian splendors that will come from a better understanding of the causes of lifestyle phenomena. Yet there is a sound basis for assuming that by struggling to demystify our ordinary consciousness we shall improve the prospects for peace and economic and political justice. If this potential change of odds in our favor be ever so slight, I think, we must regard the expansion of scientific objectivity into the domain of lifestyle riddles as a moral imperative. It's the only thing that's never been tried.

References
and Acknowledgments

Marvin Harris, et al., "The Cultural Ecology of India's Sacred Cattle." *Current Anthropology* 7 (1966), pp. 51–60. • Ford Foundation, *Report on India's Food Problem and Steps to Meet It.* New Delhi: Government of India, Ministry of Food and Agriculture (1955). • Mohandas K. Gandhi, *How to Serve the Cow: Ahmedabad.* Navajivan Publishing House (1954). • Alan Heston, et al., "An Approach to the Sacred Cow of India." *Current Anthropology* 12 (1971), pp. 191–209. • K. N. Raj, "Investment in Livestock in Agrarian Economies: An Analysis of Some Issues Concerning 'Sacred Cows' and 'Surplus Cattle.'" *Indian Economic Review* 4 (1969), pp. 1–33. • V. M. Dandekar, "Cow Dung Models." *Economic and Political Weekly* (Bombay). August 2, 1969, pp. 1267–1271. • C. H. Hanumantha Rao, "India's 'Surplus' Cattle." *Economic and Political Weekly* 5 (October 3, 1970), pp. 1649–1651. • K. N. Raj, "India's Sacred Cattle: Theories and Empirical Findings." *Economic and Political Weekly* 6 (March 27, 1971), pp. 717–722. • Stewart Odend'hal, "Gross Energetic Efficiency of Indian Cattle in Their Environment." *Journal of Human Ecology* 1 (1972), pp. 1–27.

PIG LOVERS AND PIG HATERS

The Jewish Encyclopedia (1962). • James Frazer, *The Golden Bough.* New York: Criterion Books (1959). • Mary Douglas, *Purity and Danger: An Analysis of Concepts of Pollution and Taboo.* New York: Praeger (1966). • Frederick Zeuner, *A History of Domesticated Animals.* New York: Harper and Row (1963). • E. S. Higgs and M. R. Jarman, "The Origin of Agriculture," in Morton Fried, ed., *Explorations in Anthropology.* New York: Thomas Y. Crowell (1973), pp. 188–200. • R. Protsch and R. Berger, "The Earliest Radiocarbon Dates for Domesticated Animals." *Science* 179 (1973), pp. 235–239. • Charles Wayland Towne, *Pigs, from Cave to Corn Belt.* Norman: University of Oklahoma Press (1950). • Lawrence E. Mount, *The Climatic Physiology of the Pig.* London: Edward Arnold (1968). • P. J. Ucko and G. W. Dimbleby, eds., *The Domestication and Exploitation of Plants and Animals.* Chicago: Aldine (1969). • Louise Sweet, "Camel Pastoralism in North Arabia and the Minimal Camping Unit," in Andrew Vayda, ed., *Environment and Cultural Behavior.* Garden City, N.J.: Natural History Press (1969), pp. 157–180. • Roy A. Rappaport, *Pigs for the Ancestors: Ritual in the Ecology of a New Guinea People.* New Haven: Yale University Press (1967). • Andrew P. Vayda, "Pig Complex," in *Encyclopedia of Papua and New Guinea.* • Cherry Loman Vayda, personal communication. • Some of the ideas for this chapter were first published in my column in *Natural History* magazine in October 1972 and February 1973.

PRIMITIVE WAR

Morton Fried, "On Human Aggression," in Charlotte M. Otten, ed., *Aggression and Evolution.* Lexington, Mass.: Xerox College Publishing (1973), pp. 355–362. • Andrew P. Vayda, "Phases of the Process of War and Peace Among the Marings of New

References and Acknowledgments

Guinea." *Oceania* 42 (1971), pp. 1–24; "Hypotheses About Function of War," in M. Fried, M. Harris, and R. Murphy, eds., *War: The Anthropology of Armed Conflict and Aggression.* New York: Doubleday (1968), pp. 85–91. • Frank B. Livingstone, "The Effects of Warfare on the Biology of the Human Species," in Fried, Harris, and Murphy, eds., op. cit., pp. 3–15. • Napoleon Chagnon, *Yanomamo: The Fierce People.* New York: Holt, Rinehart and Winston (1968); "Yanomamo Social Organization and Warfare," in Fried, Harris, and Murphy, eds., op. cit., pp. 109–159. • E. Richard Sorenson *et al.,* "Socio-Ecological Change Among the Fore of New Guinea." *Current Anthropology* 13 (1972), pp. 349–384. • H. C. Brookfield and Paula Brown, *Struggle for Land.* Melbourne: Oxford University Press (1963). • William T. Divale, "Systemic Population Control in the Middle and Upper Paleolithic: Inferences Based on Contemporary Hunters and Gatherers." *World Archaeology* 4 (1972), pp. 222–243, and personal communications. • William Langer, "Checks on Population Growth: 1750–1850." *Scientific American* 226 (February 1972), pp. 94–99. • Brian Spooner, ed., *Population Growth: Anthropological Implications.* Cambridge: MIT Press (1972), especially pp. 370ff. • Some of the ideas for this chapter were first published in my column in *Natural History* magazine in March 1972.

THE SAVAGE MALE

David Schneider and Kathleen Gough, *Matrilineal Kinship.* Berkeley: University of California Press (1961). • Eleanor Burke Leacock, Introduction to Frederick Engels, *The Origin of the Family, Private Property and the State.* New York: International Publishers (1972), pp. 7–67. • Marvin Harris, *Culture, Man and Nature: An Introduction to General Anthropology.* New York: Thomas Y. Crowell (1971). • Ian Hogbin. *The Island of Menstruating Men.* San Francisco: Chandler (1970). • Napoleon A.

271

Chagnon, *Yanomamo: The Fierce People*. New York: Holt, Rinehart and Winston (1968). • Johannes Wilbert. *Survivors of Eldorado*. New York: Praeger (1972). • Ettore Biocca, *Yanoama: The Narrative of a White Girl Kidnapped by Amazonian Indians*. New York: Dutton (1970). • Judith Shapiro, *Sex Roles and Social Structure Among the Yanomamo Indians in North Brazil*. Columbia University Ph.D. dissertation (1971). • Betty J. Meggers, *Amazonia: Man and Culture in a Counterfeit Paradise*. Chicago: Aldine (1971). • Jane Ross and Eric Ross, unpublished papers and personal communications. • Some of the ideas in this chapter were first published in my column in *Natural History* magazine in May 1972.

POTLATCH

Thorstein Veblen, *The Theory of the Leisure Class*. New York: Modern Library (1934). • Franz Boas, "The Social Organization of the Kwakiutl." *American Anthropologist* 22 (1920), pp. 111–126. • Ruth Benedict, *Patterns of Culture*. New York: Mentor (1946). • Douglas Oliver. *A Solomon Islands Society*. Cambridge: Harvard University Press (1955). • Ian Hogbin, *A Guadalcanal Society: The Kaoka Speakers*. New York: Holt, Rinehart, and Winston (1964); "Social Advancement in Guadalcanal," *Oceania* 8 (1938). • Marshall Sahlins. "On the Sociology of Primitive Exchange," in Michael Banton, ed., *The Relevance of Models for Social Anthropology*. London: Association of Social Anthropology Monographs 1 (1965), pp. 139–236. • Andrew P. Vayda. "A Re-Examination of Northwest Coast Economic Systems." *Transactions of the New York Academy of Sciences*, Series II, 23 (1961), pp. 618–624. • Stuart Piddocke, "The Potlatch System of the Southern Kwakiutl: A New Perspective," in Andrew P. Vayda, ed., *Environment and Cultural Behavior*. Garden City, N.J.: Natural History Press (1969), pp. 130–156. • Ronald P.

References and Acknowledgments

Rohner and Evelyn C. Rohner, *The Kwakiutl: Indians of British Columbia*. New York: Holt, Rinehart and Winston (1970). • Helen Codere, *Fighting with Property: A Study of Kwakiutl Potlatches and Warfare*. Monographs of the American Ethnological Society, 18 (1950). • Robert K. Dentan, *The Semai: A Non-violent People of Malaya*. New York: Holt, Rinehart and Winston (1968). • Richard Lee, "Eating Christmas in the Kalahari." *Natural History*, December 1969, pp. 14ff. • Marshall Sahlins, *Tribesmen*. Englewood Cliffs, N.J.: Prentice-Hall (1968). • David Damas, "Central Eskimo Systems of Food Sharing." *Ethnology* II (1972), pp. 220–239. • Richard Lee, "Kung Bushman Subsistence: An Input-Output Analysis," in Andrew P. Vayda, ed., op. cit. (1969), pp. 47–79. • Morton Fried, *The Evolution of Political Society*. New York: Random House (1967).

PHANTOM CARGO

Ronald Berndt, "Reaction to Contact in the Eastern Highlands of New Guinea." *Oceania* 23 (1952), pp. 190–228, 255–274. • Peter Worsley, *The Trumpet Shall Sound: A Study of "Cargo" Cults in Melanesia*. New York: Schocken Books (1968). • *Pacific Islands Monthly*, July 1970–April 1972. • Jean Guiart, "John Frum Movement in Tana." *Oceania* 22 (1951), pp. 165–175. • "On a Pacific Island, They Wait for the G.I. Who Became a God." *The New York Times*, April 12, 1970. • Palle Christiansen, *The Melanesian Cargo Cult: Millenarianism as a Factor in Cultural Change*. Copenhagen: Akademish Forlag (1969). • Peter Lawrence, *Road Belong Cargo*. Manchester: Manchester University Press (1964). • Glyn Cochrane, *Big Men and Cargo Cults*. Oxford: Clarendon Press (1970). • Vittorio Lanternari, *The Religions of the Oppressed*. New York: Knopf (1963). • E. J. Hobsbawm, *Primitive Rebels*. New York: W. W. Norton (1965). • Ronald M. Berndt and Peter Lawrence, eds., *Politics in New Guinea*. Nedlands:

University of Western Australia Press (1971). • Sylvia Thrupp, ed., *Millennial Dreams in Action.* The Hague: Mouton and Co. (1962).

MESSIAHS

Wilson D. Wallace, *Messiahs: Their Role in Civilization.* Washington, D. C.: American Council on Public Affairs (1943). • *The Holy Bible: Scofield Reference Bible.* New York: Oxford University Press (1945). • Salo W. Baron, *A Social and Religious History of the Jews,* second, revised and enlarged edition. 14 vols. New York: Columbia University Press. • *The Jewish Encyclopedia.* • Flavius Josephus, *The Jewish War,* translated by G. A. Williamson. Baltimore: Penguin Books (1970); *Jewish Antiquities,* translated by H. St. John Thackeray. 6 vols. London: Heinemann (1926). • Morton Smith, "Zealots and Sicarii: Their Origins and Relations." *Harvard Theological Review* 64 (1971), pp. 1–19. • William R. Farmer, *Maccabees, Zealots and Josephus.* New York: Columbia University Press (1956). • Robert Grant, *A Historical Introduction to the New Testament.* New York: Harper and Row (1963). • Erich Fromm, *The Dogma of Christ: And Other Essays.* Garden City, N.J.: Anchor paperback (1966). • Mikhail Rostovtsev, *The Social and Economic History of the Roman Empire.* 2 vols. Oxford: Clarendon Press (1957). • Michael E. Stone, "Judaism at the Time of Christ." *Scientific American,* January 1973, pp. 80–87.

THE SECRET OF THE PRINCE OF PEACE

Robert M. Grant, *A Historical Introduction to the New Testament.* New York: Harper and Row (1963); *Religion in Ancient History.* New York: Scribner (1969). • Rudolf Bultman, *Primitive Christianity in Its Contemporary Setting.* New York: World

Publishing Co. (1966). • Albert Schweitzer, *The Quest of the Historical Jesus.* New York: Macmillan (1964). • John M. Allegro, *The Treasure of the Copper Scroll.* New York: Doubleday (1964). • The Song of Victory is from George R. Edwards, *Jesus and the Politics of Violence.* New York: Harper and Row (1972). • Oscar Cullmann, *State in the New Testament.* New York: Harper and Row (1956); *Jesus and the Revolutionaries.* New York: Harper and Row (1970). • S. G. F. Brandon, *Jesus and the Zealots: A Study of the Political Factor in Primitive Christianity.* New York: Scribner (1968); *The Trial of Jesus of Nazareth.* London: B. T. Batsford (1968). • Samuel Sandmel, *The First Christian Century in Judaism and Christianity.* New York: Oxford University Press (1969). • Robert Grant, *Augustus to Constantine: The Thrust of the Christian Movement into the Roman World.* New York: Harper and Row (1970).

BROOMSTICKS AND SABBATS

H. R. Trevor-Roper, *The European Witch Craze of the Sixteenth and Seventeenth Centuries and Other Essays.* New York: Harper and Row (1969). • Henry C. Lea, *Materials Toward a History of Witchcraft.* 3 vols. Philadelphia: University of Pennsylvania Press (1939). • H. J. Warner, *The Albigensian Heresy.* New York: Russell and Russell (1967). • Jeffrey B. Russell, *Witchcraft in the Middle Ages.* Ithaca: Cornell University Press (1972). • H. Institor and J. Sprenger, *Malleus Maleficarum,* translated by the Reverend Montague Summers. London: Pushkin Press. • Michael Harner, "The Role of Hallucinogenic Plants in European Witchcraft," in Michael Harner, ed., *Hallucinogens and Shamanism.* New York: Oxford University Press (1972), pp. 127–150; *The Jívaro: People of the Sacred Waterfalls.* New York: Doubleday (1972). • Peter Furst, *Flesh of the Gods.* New York: Praeger (1972). • Julio C. Baroja, *The World of the Witches.* Chicago: University of Chicago Press (1964).

THE GREAT WITCH CRAZE

Norman Cohn, *The Pursuit of the Millennium*. New York: Harper Torchbooks (1961). • Gordon Leff, *Heresy in the Later Middle Ages*. 2 vols. New York: Barnes & Noble (1967). • George H. Williams, *The Radical Reformation*. 2 vols. Philadelphia: The Westminster Press. (1957). • John Moorman, *A History of the Franciscan Order*. Oxford: Clarendon Press (1968). • Jeffrey B. Russell, *Witchcraft in the Middle Ages*. Ithaca: Cornell University Press (1972). • H. C. Erik Midelfort, *Witch Hunting in Southwestern Germany*. Stanford: Stanford University Press (1972).

RETURN OF THE WITCH

Philip K. Bock, *Modern Cultural Anthropology*, second edition. New York: Alfred Knopf (1974). • Theodore Roszak, *The Making of a Counter Culture: Reflections on the Technocratic Society and Its Youthful Opposition*. Garden City: Anchor (1969). • Charles A. Reich, *The Greening of America*. New York: Random House (1970). • Kenneth Keniston. *Young Radicals*. New York: Harcourt Brace Jovanovich (1968). • Carlos Castaneda. *The Teachings of Don Juan*. Berkeley: University of California Press (1968); *A Separate Reality*. Simon and Schuster (1970); *Journey to Ixtlan*. Simon and Schuster (1972). • Paul Reisman, "The Collaboration of Two Men and a Plant." *The New York Times*, October 22, 1972. • Michael Harner, "The Role of Hallucinogenic Plants in European Witchcraft," in Michael Harner, ed., op. cit. (1972). • "Don Juan and the Sorcerer's Apprentice," *Time* magazine, March 5, 1973, pp. 36–45. • Philip Nobile, ed., *The Con III Controversy: The Critics Look at the Greening of America*. New York: Pocket Books (1971). • Martin Schiff, "Neo-transcendentalism in the New Left Counter-Culture: A Vision of the Future Looking Back." *Comparative Studies in Society and History* 15 (1973), pp. 130–142. • Roberta Ash, *Social Movements in America*. Chicago: Markham (1972).

About the Author

MARVIN HARRIS has taught at Columbia University since 1953 and from 1963 to 1966 was Chairman of the Department of Anthropology. He has lectured by invitation at most of the major colleges and universities in the United States. In addition to field work in Brazil, Mozambique, and Ecuador on the subjects of cross-cultural aspects of race and ethnic relations, the effects of colonialism, and problems of underdevelopment seen in ecological perspective, Harris has pioneered in the use of videotape techniques in the study of family life in this country.

Author of several books, among them the influential *Rise of Anthropological Theory: A History of Theories of Culture* and the popular undergraduate text *Culture, Man and Nature: An Introduction to General Anthropology*, Harris writes regularly for *Natural History* magazine and is a frequent contributor to the professional journals, *American Anthropologist* and *Current Anthropology*. His other books include *Cannibals and Kings* and *Cultural Materialism*.